When Women Leave Men

HOW MEN FEEL HOW MEN HEAL

STAN CHARNOFSKY

New World Library
San Rafael, California

© 1992 Stan Charnofsky

Published by New World Library
58 Paul Drive
San Rafael, CA 94903

Cover design: Brad Greene
Text design & typography: TBH/Typecast, Inc.

Library of Congress Cataloging-in-Publication Data

Charnofsky, Stan. 1931-
    When women leave men : how men feel, how men heal / by Stan
Charnofsky.
        p.   cm.
    Includes bibliographical references.
    ISBN 1-880032-01-5
    1. Men—United States—Psychology.   2. Divorced men—United
States—Psychology.   3. Single men—United States—Psychology.
4. Intimacy (Psychology)   5. Interpersonal relations.   I. Title.
HQ1090.5.U5C47 1992
158'.2—dc20   92-12117
                                                                      CIP

ISBN 1-880032-01-5

First Printing, September 1992
Printed in the U.S.A. on acid-free paper
10   9   8   7   6   5   4   3   2   1

COUNTLESS MENTORS TOUCH our lives with exquisite insights, some remembered, some absorbed unknowingly. For me, Dr. Carl Rogers is both remembered and absorbed. My deep appreciation goes to Carl, who passed away in 1987, and who once wrote:

> *People are just as wonderful as sunsets if I let them be. I don't try to control a sunset. I watch it with awe as it unfolds, and I like myself best when appreciating the unfolding of a life.*
>
> —CARL R. ROGERS
> 1902–1987

ACKNOWLEDGMENTS

A BOOK ON RECOVERY from the loss of a love is born of much pain and frustration, and with the support of many caring people.

I wish to acknowledge the insight and acumen of June Shillabeer, the courage and brilliance of my children, Kim, Dana, and Jordan, the companionship of my brother and sisters, Hal, Leonore, Charlotte, and Beatrice, and the support and affection of lovely Denice.

My appreciation to Sandy for technical assistance, and Carol LaRusso for seeing the possibilities—and for her guidance.

CONTENTS

Preface   xi

A Personal Introduction by Dick Enberg   xv

Prologue   xxi

PART ONE
SLIP-SLIDING AWAY

CHAPTER ONE
My Own Situation   3

CHAPTER TWO
Women Are Making the Move   7

   Divorce Encourages Divorce

   Competition and Intimacy

   Modern Pressures and the Death of the Dialogue

   Responsibility

CHAPTER THREE

Missing (and Spotting) the Roadsigns   19

    Sexual Roadsigns

    Tales of the Rings

    The Process of Change

CHAPTER FOUR

Forbidden Fruit   29

    Myra and Sylvan: Strangers in Paradise?

CHAPTER FIVE

Captain Romance   43

    Andy and Trudy: Dirty Old Men Need Romance Too

CHAPTER SIX

Having It Both Ways   53

    You're Right—I'm Wrong

    Did I Blow It?

    Please Hear What I'm Not Saying: Contradictory Messages

    Just Friends, Lovers No More

PART TWO
AFTER THE BREAK

CHAPTER SEVEN

The Stages   69

    Disbelief and Despair

Clutching at Straws

Depression

Resentment and Anger

Resignation and Reality

Rebirth: The First Bounce

CHAPTER EIGHT

Illustrating the Stages   93

A Weighty Problem

PART THREE

BOUNCING BACK!

CHAPTER NINE

Support Groups   109

Family

Friends

Therapy

CHAPTER TEN

New Love   121

Overcoming Distrust

The Song Is Over But the Malady Lingers On

Vulnerability and Risk

A New Freedom

CHAPTER ELEVEN

Lessons To Be Learned   133

Awareness

Expression of Feelings

Prevention Is the Cure

CHAPTER TWELVE

Surprise   143

Surprise Within Routine

Surprise Is More than Birthdays

CHAPTER THIRTEEN

An Invincible Summer   153

Omelet: American Style

Life Is What You Make It

Think Kindly on the Man

Suggested Readings   161

Some Sources on Divorce

Some Sources on Divorce and Recovery

Some Sources on Mediation

Some Sources Primarily for Men

Some Support Groups

Newer Releases

About the Author   169

Preface

I'M A MAN WHOSE MARRIAGE broke apart. This book was born out of the agony and renewal of that experience.

For ten years I have given workshops on the breakup process, about the benefits to men and women of studying and understanding the marriage-that-leads-to-divorce scenario and the rebirth that wings us back on the happiness road again. My workshop participants, mostly women, insist that what they have learned should be made available to a wider audience: men and women, married, divorced, people in committed relationships, people whose committed relationships have fizzled. So I wrote this book.

The women's movement has helped both sexes put basic human rights into perspective. The old-time double standard is diminishing, for two main reasons:

1. New opportunities.

The workplace is slowly stretching toward more equity for women, though it isn't equal yet. This has given women courage to leave unhappy or unsatisfying relationships.

2. More support.

So many people have been divorced or split apart, that women are more willing to risk that another partner will be available for them.

This book is not only for the addicted or the neurotic—for those who have debilitating life wounds. It is for my "normal" neighbor, my cousin, my friend, all of us, you. We've all been left by someone. And it doesn't feel good.

Much has been written about women (and men) who, because of childhood damage or other reasons love too much or too little, or simply the wrong way. But there are times when none of those conditions exist and our partners leave, and we are bewildered. Sometimes people do attach themselves to damaged goods, people whose lives have been marred by brutality, violence, abuse, chemicals, lost loves, pain, resentment. We must learn to enter such relationships with open eyes and full awareness. But frequently our partners are not so unusually wounded, not emotionally fragile. They struggle as you and I do to be happy and make their lives work. And when they perceive at last that their lives are not working, they leave, and understandably so.

There are self-help workshops available now for everything from "Creole Cooking" to "How to Repair Your Own TV." You can become an expert on computers, an investment entrepreneur, or a photography whiz. *Why can't you intercept and deflect the dissolution of your life's most intimate relationship?* Why haven't you become your own personal expert on love, commitment, and marriage?

By traveling along the raveled and sinuous trail of relationship endings and new beginnings in this book, you will hopefully find handles to hold onto and directions to take, in enriching your present or some future relationship. You may indeed become a modest expert on (at least your own) intimacy. Oh, how we yearn for true intimacy! And how difficult it is to establish and intricate to sustain.

As a psychotherapist working primarily with relationships, I have confronted and been challenged by hundreds of different issues that couples present. There are universal elements in all of them, yet each is unique. It is not my intent to invade people's private lives, but rather to use their experiences anonymously to get at the universals when a relationship falters. When someone says, "I don't love you anymore," or "My feelings for you have changed," we ask, what next? How come? Why?

We have missed the Roadsigns. As our road unwinds, we will explore the numerous indicators our partners might give us and why we tend to ignore them; we'll learn why we hold on to mythologies about what our partner ought to know and do; and, finally, discover how to remedy these conditions. The remedies, unfortunately, are often embraced by only one of the partners; for a relationship to flourish, however, both must master the skills.

Hopefully, this book will help both men and women comprehend the complex maze of motivations that stir a partner to close out a relationship. It is more focused on the man, however, because women leaving men is a relatively new phenomenon, men have no established emotional networks —no good place to look for solace or comfort or guidance— and, of course, I write personally from a male frame of reference.

Women have a complaint that I seldom hear from men: "Why doesn't he talk to me about his feelings? Am I supposed to read his mind?" If there is one overriding theme in this writing, it is this: the strong, silent, non-disclosing, tough, unassailable man is slowly but steadily becoming an anachronism.

This may not be easy reading for you; you may not like some of the patterns you'll find men (in the pain of their losses) or women (in their newfound determination) exhibiting. In the case studies examined here, all names have been changed. But you will recognize that men are not the more emotionally open gender. Men's emotions—other than anger —are generally more guarded and often unexpressed. Though we men feel as deeply as women, we painfully hide (and hide from) those feelings.

You may also find the remedies and solutions to breaking up, whether you are the leaving or the left partner, laborious and unappealing. It takes awareness and hard introspective work to change. Learning to create new, lasting relationships once your relationship has ended requires dramatic change.

Trust is the culprit here. When a partner has kissed you off and you've ignored the roadsigns and are caught off balance—or if you are the partner who has reached your limits and broken free—learning to trust again is like climbing Mount Everest without a rope. There are no shortcuts in this process, but hopefully this book will act as a rope.

Women, I want you to know me better, not be afraid of my hurts or put off by my caution. Though it has been said by others (and will be addressed more in Chapter Six), it merits repeating: "If you want to understand me better, please listen carefully and try to hear what I'm *not* saying, what for survival I need to say, but don't always know how to say. . . ."

In this book I speak with a man's voice. Please listen.

A PERSONAL INTRODUCTION

THIS BOOK IS ABOUT and for each man and each woman who has been hurt deeply by the loss of what they felt was a lasting relationship. In it are described the feelings and experiences of a man who has sustained a woman's announcement that she is through with him, and no longer wants to continue their relationship.

It happened to me and it happened to my friend and colleague who writes this book. It can happen in a marriage or in any love connection.

I am a former college professor, now employed as a network sportscaster. With the responsibilities of considerable long distance travel that go with my profession, many friends and associates immediately assumed that the primary reason for my divorce was that I was gone and/or too far away from home for too long. It would be nice to simplify matters with this conclusion, but it just isn't so.

What happened *between* my partner and me and what happens between a man and a woman whenever they are in contact—whether at home, on the phone, or simply in spirit—is ultimately what counts.

The focus here is on loss of a love from the man's perspective, and on the impact felt when a separation and breakup are initiated by the woman. I never conceived that divorce was imminent or could happen to me.

Feelings of loss in any dissolution are difficult enough to

comprehend and overcome, but when it strikes totally unsuspected without any preparation to absorb even the "first blow," it's a knockout from which some men might never recover. At the very best it leaves deep wounds that require much time for healing.

Rejection is no fun. Losing our children is no carnival. The implication of sexual inadequacy is no light musical comedy. Loneliness is no lark.

The author's intent in writing this book is a desire to share what some men have experienced—and learned—from the loss of a relationship. No one is exempt. Every human being is affected by the emotional trauma of loss. The woman who leaves struggles with fear of the unknown. The man who is left agonizes over his loss. We are all victims and no one wins. Part of the total experience of divorce or breakup is to recognize one's feelings, one's hurt, and one's anger. Everyone—everyone who cares—qualifies for the right to be furious! And yet the legacy is not all bleak. New life and new love do rise from the ashes.

This book does not attempt to contrive a situation with a multiple choice solution that would make it all better, or fix it. Rather, it makes explicit the feelings men might experience during the termination of a relationship. And it says, "Feel it. Understand that time is a salve and eventually you will be in a better place and able to build a new life for yourself."

I like to use the analogy of reporting a baseball game on radio-TV, where in the first inning one team has already scored ten runs. Some fans might say, "Let's turn it off now." If you feel like this, you will miss experiencing a great comeback. Stay with this game until the final exuberant end! I did, and I can tell you it's worth it. We are all part of the human predicament--in victory and defeat. And I guess the final line would be, please know that there are those who care and, as men, not afraid to open their emotions and show them to you.

The writer of this book and I began our relationship many years ago as coaches and college teachers, and as husbands. Our two families socialized often. We each had three children about the same ages. We shared with each other the way men usually share, the intimacies typically superficial, allowing ourselves to think they were deeply meaningful when they weren't.

When I was rocked with the announcement that my wife did not love me anymore, I didn't know where to go. She was not only my wife and the mother of my children, she was my only real friend. I had shut off everyone else. I had "friends" with whom we had gone to parties, or "friends" with whom to enjoy a couple of beers, but my wife was the only one I really felt I could turn to with personal matters. I desperately needed someone at least to hear me, tell me something to do, offer me some sort of magical solution that would fix the relationship. I thought of my old companion, whom I had not seen for a time. I knew he was not coaching any longer but working as a psychologist, and had his own clinic dealing with relationship problems. We had lunch together and I poured out my soul and cried, detailing my frustrations and hurts. He gave me his best clinical ear, and, at the same time, the more important gifts of warmth and love and honest caring.

A real shock for me was that one year later, his wife told him, "I don't love you anymore," and the situation reversed itself. He came to me, just as distraught, just as hurt, just as pained, feeling all the feelings that I had thought only I could feel. Here was a man who counseled those with marital difficulties every day, so I had assumed he was exempt from this sort of pain. But he showed the same despair.

I know now that no one is immune. We all can be hurt. It had even happened to a man who helps work out the conflicts of others. Perhaps because men tend to be less open with their feelings and therefore less information is shared, we make those false assumptions. This lack of real communication creates problems in man-to-man relationships—and more importantly, it has a devastating carry-over in man-woman or marital relationships.

My friend and I began truly to talk—to share aloud our common ground. We discovered amazing similarities. As we shared our pain, we found that even though we came from totally divergent directions, our concerns and problems in the separation and divorce phases had remarkably common denominators. We did the same things, and we tended to follow the same patterns as other men going through loss. We could pick up another man's comment in mid-sentence and finish it correctly. We knew what he would say!

People used to tell both of us when we were each still in our marriages, "Boy, what a great relationship you have. You and your wife are a perfect testimonial for marriage."

Yes, like fighters yet to discard their new robes, my friend and I looked great on the surface, but obviously our marriages weren't so hot. We and our wives were oblivious to the little cancers that eat away at a relationship.

The ugly twists and turns, then, of divorce are part of my experience. I have played in the Divorce League. I am a man whose woman ended our relationship. So is my friend. This book reflects those personal experiences—and those of many other men as well.

I have often admired the athlete who is a boxer. There is no single person in any athletic endeavor who is so stripped, so naked as the boxer. In many ways, I have felt like that boxer. I was alone in a squared circle. I had to protect myself, and I had to fight back. Though not specifically my story, this is the tale of men who are alone, who must protect themselves, and who must fight back.

As men whose primary relationship has ended, we become different; we are changed. It is important for men to learn to know themselves better. It is important also that women learn to know men better—that fewer secrets be kept and more open conversation occur. The bane of a solid relationship is silence. A sullen or stealthy or even a taciturn response to conflict prolongs and expands it. The harvest of conflict unresolved is dissolution.

I have heard women consistently encourage the writing of this book. One reason, I am sure, is that the place for women to find companionship, whether it be just a date or a long-lasting, committed relationship, will primarily involve contact with men who have been paired off before, the "walking wounded." Men who have gone through a breakup are very confusing. They protect themselves from reliving the hurt they experienced and build up barriers so that their feelings won't be trampled again—and therefore, they're tough to read.

This book offers a woman a chance to interpret and maybe even understand the man she is dating. We want and need to be known!

I recall early in my broadcasting career walking down a Los Angeles street. An elderly lady stopped me cold on a corner. She shook her finger at me, cocked her head and said, "I know who you are . . . I know who you are. Now, don't tell me . . . don't tell me . . . I know you . . . you're the man on the boxing . . . yes, I see you on the boxing show . . . you . . . you're uh . . . uh . . . who are you?" Still shaking her finger, she stopped and waited. I said, "I'm Dick Enberg," to which she clapped her hands and shouted,

"That's right. That's right!" She paused and with a loving smile said, "You know . . . you sure do resemble yourself."

The subject of this book is what happened to me. It is what happens to men. We do resemble ourselves.

—DICK ENBERG
RANCHO SANTA FE, CALIFORNIA

PROLOGUE

A WOMAN CAME TO ME FOR COUNSELING, woeful, dismal, her manner, voice, eyes, shoulders, manner, every aspect of her being, humbled by her recent life choices.

She had left her twelve-year marriage. What remained were two children, ages nine and six, crippling monthly bills, no job, an angry husband teetering between vindictiveness and surrender, and piercing self-doubt signaling her imminent collapse.

"And he is a nice guy," she said. "People think I've lost my mind. 'What in hell are you looking for?' they ask. 'You think there's anything better out there?' And I don't know how to answer. I think maybe I made a mistake. How will I pull it off? What if he doesn't pay support? What if I can't get a job? What if I can't find child care?"

When she finishes these questions she pauses, and a whole new set emerges.

"I left a stifling situation. But how will I know my next choice won't be worse? Do I dare trust my own judgment? Do I follow my feelings? Do I trust men? The single world out there, it's scary!"

She told me that the house had been sold.

"Yesterday," she said, "I tossed the flotsam of my last twelve years into cardboard boxes. I don't care how nice he is. I blame him for my captivity. I was a reluctant stowaway on his high seas adventure. My choice to leave was my scream for identity."

She told me that in some ways she wished he were dead. "As it is," she said, "he will always be out there, this fuzzy, distant target for my bitterness."

And then the most penetrating and desperate of all her issues: "My God, I just don't know what makes men tick!"

The image came to me of someone blindfolded at a party, spun about three times, and pushed out to seek her target.

I found myself wishing I had some simple answer to give her, some magic I could weave that would explain men and ease her troubled path—that would tear away her blindfold.

No such luck.

"Your search," I said, "is not a product. You do not awake one morning with all the pieces in place. To understand men—to understand yourself—is a process, a process you have already begun."

She smiled at me bravely, despite her pain, only dimly aware that her journey was under way.

This book can be seen as part of the process.

PART ONE

SLIP-SLIDING AWAY

Well, I have lost you; and I lost you fairly;
In my own way, and with my full consent.
Say what you will, kings in a tumbrel rarely
Went to their deaths more proud that this one went.
Some nights of apprehension and hot weeping
I will confess; but that's permitted me;
Day dried my eyes; I was not one for keeping
Rubbed in a cage a wing that would be free.
If I had loved you less or played you slyly
I might have held you for a summer more,
But at the cost of words I value highly,
And no such summer as the one before.
Should I outlive this anguish—and men do—
I shall have only good to say of you.

—EDNA ST. VINCENT MILLAY

CHAPTER ONE

My Own Situation

U P UNTIL A FEW YEARS AGO, I considered myself a relatively secure and powerful person, reasonably certain in my control over my environment, able to handle the normal and occasionally exceptional problems of
daily living. I had never really known what it was to have
unbearable pain, to suffer interminable loneliness, to feel
the deep frustration of helplessness, to live with the sense of
someone else controlling me. I had lived a relatively safe,
secure, supportive, and salutary childhood and young adult
life. And then suddenly, in my community in the San Fer-
nando Valley, came the devastating earthquake of February
9, 1971.

My family and I were thrown from our beds and knocked
to the floor. Windows broke all over the house. Walls shattered. The chimney fell over. The front door was smashed
open, its lock and bolt destroyed. The piano tipped over,
crushing its bench. After the initial shock and first series of
aftershocks, we found ourselves huddled in our pajamas,
barefoot, in the cold 6:00 A.M. wind, on the sidewalk front-
ing our house.

Fear! Cold, shivering, sleepless fear entered my life. Night
after night the aftershocks came. I was shaken from my bed
again and again. I took to keeping my clothes on the floor
and a flashlight with my shoes. I stayed up extra late at night
so my state of helplessness—being out of my clothes, in the

dark—would be brief. My security, my sense of control, my *power* began to fade.

If the very ground I stood upon became unreliable, what security could there be? I felt, for the first time in my sheltered life, a sense of utter powerlessness.

My experience—that swift shock of helplessness—is not unique. Certainly, more terrible and agonizing tales could be told. I describe this event solely to make a comparison: a few short years later, the second great shock of my life occurred. My wife of twenty years announced that our marriage was failing, that we would have to separate. Complete, utter powerlessness reigned again in my life.

That was the beginning of the most penetrating self-analysis I had ever done. People would ask me: What went wrong? Yours was such an ideal marriage, friends said. An old family friend even told me: "If we plugged you both into a computer and punched in all your variables, the two of you would come out side by side." I agreed.

And that is when I learned my first valuable generalization about relationships and breakups. There aren't very many truisms in the human relations field, but this is one:

> *It takes two people to say yes to a*
> *relationship, but only one to say no.*

Again my security was shaken. Again my world seemed uncertain, whimsical, governed by forces beyond my control. And the incongruity of it all made my life a nightmare; by all logic, the situation was a scene from Theater of the Absurd.

I could not tell you (nor could any man, I am convinced) what went wrong in my marriage. In fifteen-plus years of doing relationship counseling, I have discovered that a breakup between partners is a developmental thing. The seeds are scattered unsystematically over time. The faults are varied. Blame is a blur.

I do not know exactly what went wrong, but I do know, too late, what might have made it right: more open showing of my affection and feelings, less self-centeredness, more equitable sharing of maintenance tasks, continual affirmation of my wife's uniqueness, more willingness to admit mistakes, acceptance of her fallibility (and mine), the clear realization that perfection—in my partner, in me, or in anyone—is a myth. The words are interchangeable. The poets, writers, therapists, and gurus all seek to instruct us. We all need more of these things: Sensitivity. Communication. Attentiveness. Cooperation. Empathy.

I said that I know what *might* have made it all work out. Because despite all my adjustments, the dissolution could still have come. Intangibles, her elusive needs, society's awesome changes, the peculiar mix of energies might yet have triggered our relationship's end.

What might my wife have done to counteract the alienation, get my attention, intercept the slide toward dissolution, make the marriage work instead of giving up on it and taking that final, irreversible stand? Looking at it now, with the clarity of intervening years, I know what I would have liked—her immediate verbalizing of any resentment, physical display of affection, consultation (without being demanding) about household chores, equitable sharing of decisions about the children, and commitment to the marriage-counseling process even during the fragile, desperate final stages of the marriage—though I confess, at that time, I may not have been open to receiving them.

It would be heavenly to be wise about affairs of the heart *before* having to go through the horror of personal disaffection. Read on.

CHAPTER TWO

WOMEN ARE MAKING
THE MOVE

I N LOS ANGELES WE USED to call it the Marina/280Z syndrome. When a man reached thirty-five (or thereabouts), nagging fears about being over-the-hill encroached upon the comfortable security of his home and relationship. To prove himself one more time; to experience the variety and spice of the free and freewheeling world; to break the pattern of dull routine and the inexorable slide into middle-aged predictability: these were the priorities. The swinging bachelor scene at the Marina and the flashy sports car became the symbols. For many this was a misguided attempt to delay what is often perceived as the end of passionate sexuality. For others it was a legitimate try for happiness when the spark in a relationship fizzled.

Today the Marina plays host to both sexes. Sports cars are commandeered by women just about as often as men. Because women are just as restless, as shaken by sameness and routine, as unwilling to accept an unsupportive partnership, as fearful of the awful slip into numbness and a life of faded passion as men.

And women are making the break as often (in California, more often) as men, whether from a marriage or a committed relationship. Though fleeting youth and fear of unfulfillment and barrenness in the interaction are obvious culprits, the totality of causes is complex and deep.

One that seems obvious is that women have gradually been more accepted into the world of work and equal remuneration, so the fear of poverty and hunger for their children has lessened. Finances are powerful motivators. One man I saw in therapy complained to me that his wife, a schoolteacher, wouldn't have thought of leaving until she got tenure. That security, he told me, gave her the courage to do it. What took him many sessions to grasp was that she wanted to leave because of a flawed relationship; job security was simply the empowering event.

Divorce Encourages Divorce

Another reason, perhaps less obvious, for women taking on the risk to leave, is that prospects of loneliness and an inability to find a new partner have diminished. Divorce encourages divorce; the more people a woman sees out there, the less fearful she will be to risk a break. "I'll find someone," is her new hope. "It has to be better than what I've been in."

A couple I worked with were in what seemed like a hopeless situation. She had turned off to him totally; he had become brutal verbally and even physically abusive. Both expressed how unappealing their lives were, and how it was bound to be a better life with someone else. The singles world, from their wounded perspective, seemed positively idyllic. Ironically and surprisingly, after a couple of months of intensive work, they made the decision to stay together and work on their marriage. The man insisted the woman had changed, the woman insisted the man had. To me it meant that both wanted the relationship so long as neither was seen as the loser. And most important, the woman told me that there was still ". . . a way out," if things got too bad.

She was no longer afraid of losing the comfort and security of the marriage.

Mobility is another contributor to women leaving. With ease she can wing off to Hawaii or Mexico City with a new partner. She can remake her life quickly; the parts are interchangeable. With anonymity she can seclude herself in a dance crowd or a busy restaurant forty miles from home in forty minutes. Work keeps both men and women on the go, active, thrust together with others of both sexes in miniscenarios that resemble (but elude) intimacy. Women are as mobile, as unrestricted in their contacts, as are men.

But what cannot be changed by new locales or anonymity are the old attitudes that have developed within hurtful, damaging relationships. A woman may have the freedom to choose from all the available men out there, but her life may still be limited by the way she had to learn to live in an unloving union. And in this web of negativity men are also captive.

One man told me in therapy, "My parents were married for fifty-two years. I'm twenty-eight and I can't keep a solid relationship for more than three months. Something's wrong, something's rotten."

Another man, older and twice-married but single when he came to see me, said to me in desperation, "I've seen a lot in my fifty-six years. I've been a schoolteacher and a cab driver and I've lived with one woman for sixteen years and another for eight. But I've never seen anything like the singles scene the way it is now. I connect with a woman, we make headway, we have a little disagreement—and she's gone. Women aren't scared to be single. Leaving a relationship is about as traumatic as blowing their collective noses."

Clearly an exaggeration, yet it is obvious that staying together in a union that is troubled by conflict and criticism is no longer a viable option. Both men and women will choose a single, searching life with "possibilities" over a partnered, patterned life of friction. And while the multitude of available prospects out there does facilitate the leaving, it still does not guarantee the durability of the next connection.

Very specific negative elements constitute the residue of a broken relationship. They include *fear* of being hurt again, *caution* about commitment, *resentment* toward the opposite sex, and most of all, *mistrust* of any new entanglements.

Specific elements in a modern-day relationship will also auger trouble and precipitate breakups. One of these is the rising tide of competition between men and women in the world—and even more ominous, between loving partners.

Competition and Intimacy

Though a competitive spirit may be critical in the world of work, where winning against an adversary could contribute to one's livelihood, competition in a marital partnership is out- and-out destructive. Competition can be generated out of the frustration of unequal earning power, unequal recognition, and perceived inequality in control in the home or in the partnership. If one partner constantly perceives the other as having his way, she will incubate a percolating resentment. Where there is a winner there is a loser; where there are losers, frustration spirals and retribution simmers; where resentment and the get-even ethic operate, intimacy is lost. *Intimacy and resentment are incompatible!*

What is intimacy? It is not only, as you might think, what goes on in bed. It might be described as the opportunity to allow another person to see all the way through you without judging you, and vice versa. It is a desire to be perfectly transparent, to give yourself completely to your partner, and allow her the same transparency with you. There is wonderful joy in such a condition. There is also risk.

When partners have such intimacy, the relationship grooves. When they lose it (with competition as an active ingredient) the partnership caravan falters, is detoured, is destroyed.

Intimacy is a fragile vessel. It needs work and constant attention. It is vulnerable to a multitude of poisons. If I permit my partner to see all the way through me, I am risk-taking. I must presume her good will and affection. If her love has faded, if resentment has begun, my transparency is turned on me; my revelations are dismissed. There is no anguish more acute than your emotional disclosure answered by, "who cares?"

Any confusion about the causes of relationship decay is generated by the notion of blame. For almost every dissolution I have encountered, including my own, the temptation was to wag the finger of blame at the other. Yet blame is a smudge, based on hurt and bias, and totally unverifiable. To protect herself, a woman (or a man) will affix fault upon her partner, the most frequent message being something like: "You held me down. You kept me from reaching my potential. I was stuck with all the duties of the marriage (the practicalities of the partnership) and you had all the freedom."

If only it were so simple. Often it is society's demands that become twisted and appear to be the partner's. Or a gender role expectation gets confused with a partner's demand. I have heard men respond: "But I never kept you down. You chose to have children. You chose to stay at home. That's what your mother did. That's what your friends did. The expectation was put on you by history and your situation, not from me. Now you want to be out in the world competing and earning, and you look back and blame me for all the time you weren't. It isn't fair."

"Life isn't fair," comes the woman's answer. "I don't care how it got started, I want—I deserve—as much freedom as you. Yesterday is gone, tomorrow is too late. You've always done exactly what you want; now it's my turn."

"I didn't realize we were taking turns," the man offers with uncertainty.

"Whatever we call it," she answers, "I have the right to earn as much as you and to be recognized as much as you."

And so, for all of these reasons, valid or not, competition defeats us and intimacy is shattered.

Modern Pressures and the Death of Dialogue

What has contributed to heightened competition and its byproduct, lost intimacy, is an awareness by some women (and the fear of some men) that other women are becoming independent and self-supporting. The women's movement has educated women to sisterhood. What might have been an uncomplicated state of affairs thirty years ago—a committed relationship, at that time usually marriage—has become a union fraught with pressure, temptation, and pitfalls. Our roles are unclear, our duties muddled. The contracts need renegotiation.

There are different pressures today; open dialogue seems difficult. But don't presume that all committed relationships were joyful and tranquil "in the old days" and have simply gone to hell in a handbag today. There is ample evidence that the old lump-in-the-throat "normalcy" (as portrayed in shows like *Father Knows Best, The Waltons,* and *Little House on the Prairie*) were distortions, at best.

A 1980 article in the *New Yorker* cited Billy Gray, the actor who played brother Bud in *Father Knows Best* in the '50s, as feeling "ashamed" that he ever had anything to do with the show. He described it as "totally false," the all-wise father returning each evening to his white frame home, flitting through the front door and gurgling, "Margaret, I'm home." It caused many Americans to feel inadequate, that their own lives couldn't measure up to that ideal, the "way it was supposed to be."

The fact that between 1960 and 1980 there was a 100% increase in the divorce rate is not attributable to changes in divorce laws, which were not greatly liberalized, but rather to new definitions of family perfection. Such criteria as fun, love, feeling good, and towering orgasms became the priorities for relationships to endure. Old-time unions may not have been perfect, but changed definitions of perfection in marriage are part of the cause of today's malaise.

Today's man-woman partnership, (a marriage or an exclusive relationship) is characterized by a privacy unknown many years ago. When the predominate family unit lived in smaller, rural communities, "bad" behavior was public knowledge. Neighbors were often privy to family affairs. Today we possess more anonymity; we hardly know our neighbors, and they hardly know us.

In the past, open dialogue was more a matter of routine, between families, among neighbors. As more isolated family structures have developed, such dialogue waned. And it waned simultaneously within the single relationship as well. Privacy began to imply seclusion, even secrecy, in thoughts and feelings, even from your most intimate partner.

There are several complicated reasons for dialogue to deteriorate in a relationship. Here are three:

1. Open dialogue has become a victim of resentment.

One partner feels ignored, unnurtured. She confronts her man openly and cleanly with her anger and frustration and needs. But he, guarded, masculine fellow, retreats into silence. Time and again she approaches, and time and again he retreats. At last, resentfully, she changes her tactics; she delivers the raised eyebrow, the tossed shoulder, and ultimately, the anguishing, "who cares?"

2. Open dialogue has become a victim of images.

When a man insists on maintaining a stance of invulnerability, the give and take of productive dialogue is lost. We men will often show our anger—an acceptable male, adult expression—but seldom our fear, pain, grief, or even our joy. For dialogue does not only consist of words; the most poignant sign of intimacy can be a nod of silent understanding across a crowded room. An obvious example of fresh appreciation for your partner is an unsolicited and savory squeeze at a family gathering. Yet a frequent complaint from women in counseling is: "He only shows affection when it leads to sex. It makes me feel he only cares about me for my body."

3. Open dialogue has become a victim of criticism.

Both men and women get caught up by the old adage, "familiarity breeds contempt." In my counseling practice, I have listened to many couples bury themselves in verbal graveyards, dead-ends that leave both partners defensive and wounded. Relationships are plagued by what have come to be known as "You" messages, comments such as, "You're

crazy," or "You're the one who won't listen," or "You're becoming impossible to live with." The "I" response, a clear
expression of personal feelings rather than criticism or accu-
sations, is the better alternative—and the hardest thing for
couples to learn.

◆ ◆ ◆

In counseling, I will respond to a vituperative "You" comment from one partner to another with: "There isn't another
person in the world you would talk to that way. Did you hear
what you just said to your partner?"

Here's an example of a typical dialogue between a couple.

One client turned to his wife and said, "So what do you
want from me? Look at you. You're not the girl I married.
You're a blimp, a fat blimp. How could I be turned on to you?
When are you going to lose weight? Where's the sweet, thin,
affectionate girl I married?"

"Listen Carl," she replied, crunching down hard on his
name, "I'm not a girl, see, Carl. I'm a woman, Carl. And I'll
lose weight when I feel like it. Why should I show you affection? What do you do for me? You're so self-centered, Carl,
that you can't think of anyone but yourself. When are you
going to examine your priorities, Carl?"

And at last, when they paused for breath, I was able to
say, again, "I swear, there isn't another person in the world
you would talk to that way." Five months later, Carl's wife
asked him to leave, and Carl told me he was surprised.

What is most sad to me is when one of the partners gets
the idea of using "I" messages, but the other doesn't. This
skill demands mastery by both partners if the dialogue is to
work. One of my clients from another culture once told me,
in halting English (in front of her husband), "I try this. I say

to him how I feel. I do it for years. I try to be good listener. When it comes my turn to talk, he is bored. He watches the TV. His eyes go there even when he starts to listen. Never do I get my wants." And the man, squirming, red-faced, answered only, "Ah, what do you want from me? Always complain, complain."

Though it may be an obvious piece of advice, try to remember that *open dialogue is the key to the survival of any relationship.*

Responsibility

I do not, in relationship counseling, talk about fault or blame. I talk about responsibility. Both partners are responsible for a relationship in which dialogue diminishes. Both partners must be held responsible for stating, openly and clearly, their needs and wants. Neither partner can be responsible for, or in charge of, the other person's happiness. But both are responsible for—and will suffer the consequences of—old feuds never resolved.

But becoming aware of your own personal limits, the final, uncompromising reality that you can't take it any longer, will happen differentially. That is, one partner almost always reaches that awareness at a different time than the other.

It often takes the first partner many painful months, possibly years, of building up courage and resources—or enough anger and resentment—to make the final statement, to take the ultimate stand, though it may seem sudden, an unexpected bolt out of the blue, to the other. One partner is all it takes to decide a relationship is over. But both are culpable; both are responsible.

And that brings us to the second valuable generalization about break-ups:

*In every troubled partnership, there are
inescapable, blatant, neon roadsigns
flashing out warnings: "Problems ahead,
relationship in danger."*

But in our lassitude, or our oblivious preoccupation with life's duties and pleasures, we ignore them. And for good reason. It is easier and less threatening to be irresponsible. Roadsigns that tell of human-to-human friction are scary, so we don't read them, run away from them, do not feel the heat of them. FEEL them, ah, there's the rub. Do we men run from what we feel? Do we take responsibility for what we feel?

When a woman says to her man, "I just don't feel very warmly toward you tonight," is that feeling simply to be dismissed by her partner, his response a critical, "Don't be so bitchy." When she says, night after night, "I'm tired, I'm going to sleep," should that be left at that, an inevitable condition of the lifelong partnership? Shouldn't both partners be *responsible* for confronting such a failed dialogue?

There are many culprits in the development of relationship disharmony. We have toured some of them and come now to a more in-depth look at those roadsigns.

CHAPTER THREE

MISSING (AND SPOTTING) THE ROADSIGNS

S INGERS BARBRA STREISAND and Neil Diamond tried to set us straight a while back with their song about the things that don't happen anymore when a relationship sours. You turn out the light, the flowers stop coming, the love songs get sung to someone else. Joy erodes.

Among the things that are lost in the toppling of a marriage or a partnership, there are more than niceties. You have missed seeing the tangible, iridescent roadsigns—things that have happened—that were flashing out important messages. The fact that we could ignore them is a monumental tribute to the male ego, to blindness, preoccupation, even stupidity, and ultimately, fear. Cut away the foliage from the masculine forest of toughness, and we are left with the bleak, disquieting realization that we did not read the roadsigns because we were afraid to.

Suddenly, startlingly, when the crisis hits, all the unfinished business that had been cavalierly swept under the carpet puffs back out in a great cloud of conflict that plagues and envelops us. And, incredibly, in our blind preoccupation, and in our fear, we might even assume once again that this too will pass; trouble, yes, but not enough to scuttle the relationship, confrontation, of course, but not unlike others we'd had. Our carpet is big. And it's just too darned scary to look under it.

Sexual Roadsigns

The sexual roadsigns are usually the most vivid and in retrospect the most hurtful; they represent rejection at the deepest point of intimacy, an attack on your peak vulnerability. It is a powerful realization that, though relationship discord may not start out in bed, it always ends up there.

HANK'S STORY

Hank came to see me in therapy. His sixteen-year marriage was a shambles. Immediately, he broke all the rules of masculinity by allowing tears to show.

Attractive, fortyish, decidedly athletic, he had not allowed his body to go to fat. The anguish of his defeat humbled him; his body drooped.

"About three years ago it started. Her sexual reaction to me was dutiful. It got so I didn't want to initiate anything. When I did, she would lie there like a log. I said angry things to myself many times, but I was afraid if I said it to her she would shut me out altogether. And then finally I just made the decision that it was stupid for me to try to make love to her when she didn't seem to care about it. So for about the last two years we have had sex only when she wants it—like maybe once every ten days. But now, when it's too late, I realize that that's even tougher on me.

"I just wait there in bed, see, and she's in the bathroom. When she comes out I sniff the air to see if she's put on any perfume. That's my clue, the perfume. It means she's willing—or I guess that she's made the choice—to get it on. Shit, it's been so degrading."

His eyes moistened, and then valiantly, with a brittle swallow, he choked the tears away.

"You saw all those signs but did nothing," I responded softly.

"Well, what could I do? Oh, I mean, she told me I was irritable and bossy, and that I didn't support her emotionally. Well, hell, she started it with all that manipulation in the bedroom. Anyway, I wasn't doing anything on purpose."

I looked at Hank curiously. Of course he had not done anything on purpose. He was wounded by frustration and neglect. His wife was wounded by frustration and neglect. She had shown her hurt angularly, by withholding her favors, instead of crisply and directly. And he had absorbed the pain silently, stoically, ignoring the portents.

Hank is one of a growing number of men who discover too late that remaining silent about changes in the intensity of intimacy in a partnership guarantees them an inevitable and unpalatable trip into single life. And many women have come to realize that in withholding their sexuality from their men they deprive themselves as well, and resentment spirals.

MORT'S STORY

Mort came in complaining about not having had oral sex with his wife for the past seven years. But that chronic absence in their sexual routine soon proved not to be the only culprit. He was now living in an apartment, after his wife asked him to give her some space

21

and a chance to get her feelings sorted out. It had come as a surprise to him, though the events leading up to that move might have offered ample warning, had he not absorbed them resignedly as a condition of his static marriage.

"We've been married twenty-one years," he said. "We were kids when we tied the knot. She was so open and free. God, how it's changed."

Curiosity won out over my therapist model, and I uncharacteristically plied him with questions. "What changes, what do you mean, how is she different and how are you different?"

"Well, I mean in the last few years she seems to have gotten cooler and more shy, at least with me. When our last child was born she nursed him for a year, and whenever she would go to bed she would keep her bra on. That part of her body was reserved, and not for me. And where she used to display her body—and we'd both run around naked a lot—now she dresses and undresses in the bathroom.

"The oral sex is another part of it. All of a sudden she finds that distasteful. Well, after you've had it and then you don't get it anymore it becomes like a fantasy. You know, you build it up in your mind as the highest point of passion. I've been faithful, but don't think I haven't considered straying. Anyway, now *she* wants out, can you believe that? With all of her physical rejection of me, now she wants out!"

"And with all those indications that something was wrong between you, what did you do about it?" I asked.

"Oh, I didn't really do anything. I thought she was going through some mid-life crisis or something. I mean, we agreed on politics and religion and child-rearing and stuff like that, so I figured we'd stick it out for sure and maybe she'd get over her weird moods. Look where that strategy's got me."

Indeed, where had that strategy got him? Into therapy and, ultimately, divorce court.

What Mort did not understand was that his wife had felt rejected too, not the way he had, physically, in the bedroom, but emotionally, in terms of camaraderie, in their spiritual lives, and in their dialogue.

When a partner says to her husband, "You know I don't like it when you kiss me on the neck," is that a harsh but unmistakable roadsign? ("She used to love it when I kissed her on the neck.")

One man told me: "When we make love—have sex—she turns her face and won't kiss me."

Another said: "Every night, when we go to bed, my wife turns her back to me and lies on her side. All I ever see is a big rear end under the covers."

Another told me, with bittersweet humor: "My wife always signed her notes and letters with a little heart. Now she puts the heart on notes to the milkman or the piano tuner, but not to me."

There are hundreds of examples, but perhaps the most hurtful was this anecdote: "Right in the middle of love-making, just at the moment of orgasm, I said to her, 'How can I get more of you?' and she answered, detached, miles away, 'Go with me to marriage counseling.' She stunned me in my most exposed moment. But I took it in resignedly as a condition of our marriage."

Tales of the Rings

One indirect, yet extremely common roadsign has to do with third-finger-left-hand rings. Almost every man has a "tale of the ring."

When you fall in love with a woman you ply her with gifts, the ultimate being a ring as a pledge of love and loyalty. It is a symbol of commitment. Some time ago, women began to reciprocate; mutual commitment was sealed by an exchange of rings.

When love begins to fail, the ring begins to oppress. It is a chafing reminder of painful moments, unsettled conflicts, the souring of dreams, the detour of hope. It is no wonder that a woman—in a love gone wrong—would want to cleanse herself of that peripatetic and constant reminder. What happens most often is that the ring, and its removal, becomes an *indirect* message, or roadsign, pointing towards the demise of a good relationship.

PHILLIP'S STORY

Phillip, thirty-six and married for fourteen years, described his tale of the ring: "About two years before our marriage ended, my wife stopped wearing her ring. I asked her about it and she told me she had pain in her fingers, arthritis or something. Yet she would wear cocktail rings, you know, on other fingers. My next question, 'You have arthritis only in the third finger, left hand?' was not appreciated. I thought maybe she was getting into women's lib and the ring was a symbolic shackle to her—so I ignored it."

24

RON'S STORY

Ron, who had been a skilled athlete in his younger years, told me, "She stopped wearing her ring. In sixteen years I hadn't taken my ring off once. Ball games, tennis, swimming—it didn't matter. When I see no ring on her left hand I ask her, 'What's happening?' and she says the ring represents ownership to her, and she was a free agent. Hell, it never used to. It didn't represent ownership to me. Now I can see it was symbolic. She was trying to tell me something. Then I tried to get my ring off and it wouldn't come off. I soaped it and greased it . . . hell, I almost chopped it off. And when I finally tore it away from my skin, I was so mad I wanted to throw it off the hill behind my house. But some spark, some stubborn hope nagged at me and I stashed it in a jar in my bedroom. A lot of good it did me."

Ron's marriage ended seven months later. Oddly, when he stood in court for the final decree, his wife approached him and said she loved him and would always love him—but being married to him had become unworkable and impossible.

Two messages are being delivered when a partner abandons a love token such as a wedding or commitment ring. One is: My love for you has dwindled; I feel distant and alienated. The other is: I don't feel comfortable telling you this directly.

If your woman begins to distance herself from you symbolically, are you open and courageous enough to challenge the implication? Are you willing—without a punishing intent—to confront her action with questions and information that could unmask the painful but very necessary truth?

Only through direct and pointed dialogue can the decline of a relationship—and its myriad slanted miscommunications—be averted. The missing of roadsigns is a universal affliction, primarily because of our fear of conflict and loss. The status quo, even if unappetizing, is generally perceived as preferable to the unknown—which could mean aloneness, emptiness, and emotional anguish. So we stonewall the obvious, and miss the inevitable.

Spotting roadsigns is the alternative—spotting them and reacting to them. Despite the powerful inertia of a failing relationship, tracking down the roadsigns early enough can lead to a successful process of change.

The Process of Change

Psychiatrist Alan Wheelis in his book, *How People Change*, writes that the quintessential ingredient in change is suffering. When one suffers, one is open to change. The three steps that then follow sequentially are: *awareness*, *desire*, and *action*. When one partner, and here we'll say the woman, becomes aware that she is suffering, she incubates a smoldering desire, which ultimately erupts into painful but courageous action. She demands change. She demands her freedom. Like Isadora Wing in Erica Jong's *Fear of Flying*, she refuses any longer to be the back two legs of a couch.

Awareness is the key step—the process that counselors focus on—and no lasting change occurs without it. But *desire* is also vital, and *action*—new action in a new direction.

Here's an example: If I point out to you that you are biting your fingernail, you become aware of it and can take it out of your mouth. If you stop by chance, and do not know why you did, you will probably start again. But the second step, desire, is indispensable also, because even with awareness you could respond, "I know it," and continue to bite—unless the desire to change is also cultivated. And finally, if in the instant the old behavior is about to begin you take a different action instead, you achieve a different, a changed result. The first time you take new action is the hardest. It means shattering a familiar pattern. The second time is easier, and the third time easier yet, and so on, until a new pattern exists.

In a relationship that is disintegrating, awareness is the only possible intercepter—for both the woman and the man. As the woman becomes aware of her suffering, the man must become aware of the roadsigns. If both are aware, in time—if both retain "goodwill" or desire—the dialogue can open up, a new pattern can emerge, and the partnership be saved. One of the first questions I ask a couple when they come together for counseling is, "Does each of you have the desire to work on this relationship? If not, your honesty can save all of us a lot of time; if so, we have much hard work to do on the difficult task of change."

Change is not an instantaneous process. Even with all the steps in place, it is painful and slow to reach the point of new action. Old habits—old protections—are like old companions, and disengage reluctantly. Roadsigns are stark notices that a relationship has decay, and that decay produces ugly consequences.

CHAPTER FOUR

FORBIDDEN FRUIT

THERE COMES A TERRIBLE TIME in the long deterioration of a relationship when sex is abandoned, more often than not by the woman's choice. It makes sense—who wants to make love when love has faded? but it is nonetheless painful and even humiliating. Some men feel a loss of masculinity, feel degraded. Many turn angry and punishing. Almost all become aware of a desperate erotic longing for the very woman who is rejecting them. When a man has experienced high and powerful moments with a woman and she is suddenly no longer available, she becomes like forbidden fruit, curious, mysterious, and alluring.

This is true not only for the sexual parts of a relationship but all aspects. Men may be surprised to discover that, even though their relationship has been unhappy and they have been angry and frustrated and irritated—though these moods predominate—when their women leave, they suffer deeply over lost moments of togetherness, vanished contacts, forbidden intimacies.

What is obvious, but is unnoticed by most men, is that the loss had been incremental, progressing over time, slowly but steadily. When your partner says the piercing words that make the break, she has already been forbidden to you in multiple ways. Her affections have already been withheld, her emotional availability to you severely diminished. It is the stark reality of the actual pronouncement—the putting words to it—that turns the spotlight on your faded intimacy.

You have been silently, perhaps unknowingly, mourning your loss for some time. Now it is in the open.

Now that you cannot have your partner—and you have been physically faithful—what do you do? You realize you love her, you struggle with loneliness, and you ache physically for her touch, her warmth, her body close to yours. You are in a condition that could be labeled a *one-sided addiction*. The tendency now is to overestimate your own sexual appeal and to underestimate your partner's resolve. Some therapists call this *denial*, others *fantasizing*.

"I'm a great lover: She won't find anyone else like me. She'll miss what I give her." An overemphasis is placed on the sexual part of the relationship, a distortion, many times, as the woman looks at it. She is likely to say: "Our sex fell apart because *we* fell apart."

The temptation then is to drown the pain, to seek solutions outside yourself. If you turn to alcohol or drugs, you become a double loser. If you turn to casual sexual encounters, you face new, more terrifying possibilities—infection, illness, death, or being lured and hurt again.

The following case example, while it does end positively, illustrates the awesome risk that accompanies a careless turning outward, the seeking of instant gratification to salve the wounds of loss.

Myra and Sylvan: Strangers in Paradise?

Background

Here is a seventeen-year marriage. Sylvan is ten years older than his wife. They were thirty and twenty when they married. Sylvan is cautious about showing emotion, expressing anger easily, but little else. Myra stayed at home for the first twelve years of the marriage, the primary nurturer for their daughter and two sons, now fifteen, fourteen, and ten. When Josh, the youngest, was five, Myra took a part-time job as an assistant prereschool teacher. She has worked for the last five years, and two years ago went back to college to finally finish her bachelor's degree in child development.

When they came to see me for couples counseling, Myra said, "Sylvan has always been stiff and unexpressive. When I was a kid I took it—maybe I wasn't even aware—but now I want more. I've been learning about my own emotions and I want him to be freer to show his." Sylvan said: "This isn't the girl I married. She's changed. She was always, as the song says, as soft and as pink as a nursery. Now she's hard, demanding. I don't even enjoy coming home from work."

I spent three months working with Myra and Sylvan as a couple, learning much about their styles and personalities. They were very different. I tried to comprehend what might have brought them together to start with, but too much time had elapsed, too much change had occurred. Myra seemed driven, hungry, as if she had hooked into some elemental truth about herself and the world, and could not rest from its pursuit. Sylvan seemed wounded, resentful, betrayed by what he seemed to view as a breach in the marriage contract. His was an old- fashioned view, hers a newer, emerging one.

If they could only get back to the early attractions between them, I thought—if they could, as the saying goes, rekindle the spark. Lots of ifs.

The alternative would be for Sylvan to change—no easy task—and to accept the "new" Myra as she was becoming.

And even then, the question was, would Myra stay with Sylvan, or had her new momentum taken her beyond this relationship?

To my surprise, Sylvan made a move. He called me on a Sunday evening to cancel our Monday appointment. "I'm moving out tomorrow," he said. "I've had enough criticism. If she doesn't like me the way I am, somebody else will."

He left on a Monday. Two weeks later on a Monday, a woman whom I came to know only as Susie moved in with him. I learned later that Sylvan had begun to see Susie several weeks before leaving his home. While initially caught off guard, Myra pulled herself together and in a few days acclimated herself to a new single life with her children. She continued to see me in therapy, while Sylvan terminated his sessions with me.

Divorce is a process, not an event. The couple began counseling in hopes of rescuing a struggling relationship, but the task became one of learning to let go and to renew.

Three more months passed, and one morning I received a call from Sylvan seeking an appointment. Myra had already filed for divorce and had told me that Sylvan seemed indifferent. I assumed there was some new development.

Single Time

A brief excerpt from our first renewal counseling session:

Sylvan: It's been great. My new lady, Susie, doesn't criticize me. The sex has been fabulous. I've been thinking I really made the right move.

Counselor: You sound up, enthusiastic—yet you're here for some reason.

Sylvan:	Well . . . I mean, there are some adjustments. I miss my kids. (Long pause.) If Myra hadn't been so critical of me. . . .
Counselor:	Having some second thoughts?
Sylvan:	Oh no. Hell no. (Pause.) Damn it, I am angry at her. It's her fault I had to leave my home, leave my kids.
Counselor:	I hear your anger, all right. And your finding fault too.
Sylvan:	I may not be the most flexible guy, but her wants were unreasonable. She expected me to change overnight. How about her? It took her all those years to change. How could she expect me to be different on demand?
Counselor:	So her expectations were unreasonable. Yet, you're the one who left, who made the move.
Sylvan:	I couldn't stand it any more! I'd come home and she'd be off to class somewhere—my daughter's in charge—or she'd be having coffee with some guru she discovered.
Counselor:	You were worried she was growing apart from you, maybe even looking to develop a new relationship?
Sylvan:	Hell, she denied it, said I was foolishly jealous. But I think she enjoyed bending me out of shape—showing me what a liberated woman she was. Could you have just locked your mouth and taken that shit?
Counselor:	So you decided to get out, to break it off?

> Sylvan: I need some affection. There are still women out
> there who want to please a man. Susie is one.

Although it was difficult for him, intermixed with denial, Sylvan tentatively admitted his hurt and his needs for nurturance. Anger still dominated as his primary expressive emotion. What he had not yet learned—was not yet aware of—was that anger *is almost always a secondary emotion.* We feel hurt but ignore it and show anger instead; or we feel fear and ignore it and show anger; or we feel resentment, but show only our anger.

Sylvan came in again one week later. Myra had told me during the week that Sylvan had called her every day, stopped over twice, shouted at her, and accused her of ruining his life—the last in front of their ten-year-old son. Here is the transcript of a brief part of the second session:

> Sylvan: Susie's prettier than Myra and younger and a
> wildcat in bed. Why would I ever think of going
> back?
>
> Counselor: Why would you?
>
> Sylvan: I wouldn't. (Pause.) Not the way Myra is now.
> (Pause.) Susie's a little strange. I mean the way
> she lives. Likes to go dancing a couple times a
> week. Likes to go out for sushi a couple times
> a week. When she eats she never sits down—
> always on the run.
>
> Counselor: These are not your ways of doing things.
>
> Sylvan: Oh, it's not so bad. I'm learning there are other
> ways to be. What Myra and I used to do had
> become static. The fun had gone out of things.

Counselor: You'd forgotten how to play.

Sylvan: You said it. (Pause.) Susie's a little bizarre, but she's good for me. Right now she's good for me.

I was aware that Sylvan had begun to miss the patterns of his many years of marriage. The novelty in the new relationship was already wearing off. His longing for familiarity came through despite denial. I was pretty sure by now that Susie would turn out to be a "transitional person" in Sylvan's life. It was also apparent that Sylvan (and Myra) were becoming aware that the idea of play in their lives had long been moribund. Four weeks later:

Sylvan: I'm not going to stay with Susie. Something's not right. She's too . . . too unpredictable. I need some stability in a relationship, someone I can count on.

Counselor: And you can't count on Susie.

Sylvan: Don't get me wrong. The excitement is there and the sex part is great. I mean, I want to stay in touch with Susie, go out with her and all that, but I just . . . I just can't live with her.

Counselor: It seems as if you love the playful part with Susie, it's the more serious part, the business part that bothers you.

Sylvan: I jumped in too fast. I guess I needed some affection, somebody who wasn't always on my case. But being with someone in the quiet times, weeknights or mornings or Sunday afternoons—you've got to have some kind of connection.

Counselor:	Intimacy is a lot more than sexual passion. Compatibility carries over into lots of areas. Is that what you're saying?
Sylvan:	Sure. (Pause.) I think Myra has a boyfriend. Some faggy guy with a Mercedes.
Counselor:	You sound angry at him.
Sylvan:	I knew she wouldn't be alone for long. All that phony independence. Well, I shouldn't be angry at him. He's somebody new. It's Myra I'm pissed at.
Counselor:	Is there something explicit you'd like to say to Myra?
Sylvan:	Yeah. Yeah, I'd like to tell her that she's not gonna find someone like me so easily. That she can't replace me. That a fancy car or gourmet dinners don't substitute for a loyal partner—or for years of struggling together to make things work. She'll find out. She'll find out. . . .
Counselor:	You seem to believe that Myra is reaching for the superficial, while you want something more enduring.
Sylvan:	Oh, I'm no saint. I'm gonna play for a while. Why not? It's a candy store out there. I'm still young and the pretty girls still look at me. (Pause.) If only Myra could see what they see. (Laughter.) It's been a long time. I feel like a stranger in paradise.
Counselor:	It's okay for you to play but not Myra?
Sylvan:	Hell, she can play. (Here he stops and begins to cry. I wait for him, and after a moment he con-

tinues in a different tone, less defiant, clearly more vulnerable.) She brings a new guy into *my* house with my kids there. When I have the kids he spends the night. In *my* bed! (Pause.) I feel like a child, driving by the house, looking for the guy's car. I torture myself. I want her so much. It doesn't make sense.

Counselor: You can't take her criticism of you, so you move out, and now the consequences of that move are painful, even torturous. You certainly seem as if you're having second thoughts.

Sylvan: (He cries, embarrassed, with his hand over his face, then catches his breath.) I can't go back. I'm not even sure she would take me. She's going on with the divorce. She ignores all the things we had, the things we did. The vacation in Mexico, the time we pulled together when we had a fire in our garage, the birth of our children. She forgets those things. Or, she doesn't care. It feels too late to me. . . .

Counselor: Too late.

Sylvan: I mean, I think it's over. She shows no compassion, no sentiment or nostalgia about our life together.

Counselor: All those years, all those memories, and nothing moves her.

Sylvan: I've got to go on. Find some new people. Myra had all the friends. I gave mine up when we got married. Why do men do that?

Counselor: Your question is difficult. I wonder if most men ever have true friends to start with.

Sylvan: Well, I don't. Everybody I know is married. I woke up the other morning and realized, all our neighbors, all the people we'd have dinner with or go to the movies with, are all married couples who are Myra's people, not mine. I don't really have anyone.

Counselor: You want a new support system.

Sylvan: I need people in my life. It's terrible to be alone.

Terrible to be alone. Sylvan had come to understand that, not only intellectually, but in the gut. His first tendency was to demean others: Myra for her choices, the new man for his affluence, even himself for his vulnerability and pain. But then, in the safe emergency of the therapeutic session, he got clear, reconsidered. He understood that the new man was innocent and struggling to find intimacy just as he was. His discontent focused then on Myra and how misguided her actions were. And finally, he allowed himself to feel deeply the hurt that gnawed at him—and to show it even in the presence of another man.

The wish that he could return to his old life grew stronger, especially when he realized he had no close friends, no solid support system. He was beginning to clutch at straws when he wished that Myra could see him as some of the single, pretty women do. The tendency at this point was to forget the dissonance that led to the separation in the first place, forget that the intimacy in his marriage had withered. All the old tender moments began to invade, all the poignant memories. And the loss then feels overwhelming. This is the period of depression, when all hope for resurrection of the marriage begins to dissolve.

Sylvan began to try himself out on different people, play the field, sample, as he put it, the candy store goodies. Four weeks passed and he called me on the morning of our scheduled evening appointment, quite distraught, asking if I could see him right then, at that moment. I learned in this session that the usual "bouncing-back stages" that I would expect Sylvan to enter, anger and resentment, and on into resignation and reality, probably weren't going to happen.

> Sylvan: (Appearing pale, agitated.) I'm in deep trouble. I got involved with an actress—not famous but she works occasionally in the soaps, bit parts, commercials. We had sex three or four times, then it ended. Then I started seeing a woman I've known through work, a salesperson. We wanted to make love, but she insisted I get a blood test, you know, for AIDS, 'cause I told her I'd had a couple of other relationships since Myra. (Pause.) I had the test. . . . (He leans his head on his hand, bowed, sagging.) It came out positive.

I was silent, allowing him to stay with his pain a moment, while conjuring up challenges to his information. Finally I spoke softly with, I believe, honest affection:

> Counselor: Are they sure? Can there be a mistake?
>
> Sylvan: I'm gonna take another test, more comprehensive. But I'm scared.
>
> Counselor: Of course. Of course you are.
>
> Sylvan: I did the wrong thing leaving Myra. Things weren't that bad. I wanted to play for a while, legitimately, that's all.

Counselor: You made the logical move as you saw it. Now, with hindsight you're looking at different motives, questioning your choice.

Sylvan: It was a mistake. The world is different now. Look what it got me. Now I don't have Myra and . . . and I'm gonna die!

Counselor: Your sexual adventures and your decision to leave Myra—those seem like independent acts to me.

Sylvan: (Angry at me now.) I moved out! Nothing would have happened to me if I'd have stayed in the house. Now my children won't have a father.

When he left my office he was staggering, defeated. He did not tell Myra his catastrophic news, but in her own way, she must have sensed something, because in her meeting with me she reported him seeming distracted and morose when he came for the children.

Ten days passed and I got a phone message from Sylvan. When I returned the call, he answered. I said my name and a screech battered my ear, followed by "The test was negative. Negative. The first one was all wrong. The lab technician blew it. I'm okay. I'm not sick. I'm not dying!"

He made an appointment for the next evening.

Sylvan: What a perspective you get when you think you've bought the store.

Counselor: A kind of desperation.

Sylvan: Exactly. Oh man, was I scared. (Pause.) I'll tell you, I've learned my lesson.

Counselor: Learned . . .

Sylvan: (Interrupting.) It's a serious world out there. It's not all fun and games. Used to be you saw something you liked and you went for it. Now you gotta have an inquisition first. And it's not just if she's clean and you're clean—it's everybody she's been with and everybody you've been with.

Counselor: It's like a halter. Your freedom is restricted.

Sylvan: I was agonizing over whether it was Susie or my actress who did me in. You wouldn't believe the thoughts I had about them. Now my new friend and I are free to go for it—you know, the woman at work.

Counselor: That's a nice feeling isn't it? You're out there, you found someone you like, you've checked it out, and you're able to go ahead with no inhibitions.

Sylvan: No inhibitions. Freedom. Yeah, it is a nice feeling. You know, I think I'm gonna stop seeing you for a while. If something comes up I'll give you a call—I won't forget your number.

Recovery Time

Sylvan did not call me for nearly four months. I wondered about him, whether his near-tragedy had transformed him in some lasting way. In his final session with me, he'd seemed on a kind of equilibrium, but I wasn't sure if it would be temporary, a product of supreme relief, or a more durable condition which would help him get on with his life.

Myra stopped seeing me at about the same time, pleased, as far as I could tell, with herself as a single mother and an assertive, achieving person. Her relationship with the Mercedes man seemed tenuous to me, but she behaved as if it met her needs for the moment.

When Sylvan did call, his news surprised me. He did not need to see me, he said, but considering how much work we had done together he thought I'd like to know that he and Myra were back together. I asked him at whose instigation and he answered, "Both." Myra called me a few days later and said that the single world was a risky and unsatisfying arena, that Sylvan had told her all about his scare, and that she thought Sylvan had changed dramatically. Now she could pursue her own goals and still stay in the familiar marriage. She was *hoping* (and she stressed that word) that Sylvan would be more self-disclosing and emotionally open. Although, she added, of that she could not be sure.

As I pondered the outcome of this interesting and volatile case, I concluded that bouncing back from the loss of a relationship can literally mean bouncing *back*—into the same relationship. Fear is a powerful motivator.

Forbidden fruit is *any* unattainable desire. In men-women relationships, it has the potential to drive us mad—and to drive us into foolish and perilous adventures. When your woman backs away, there is no way to eliminate viewing her as someone rare and splendid, all the old passion gets exaggerated in its splendor, the possibility of fulfillments distorted.

But aside from the erotic desperation that comes with a lost love, our need (yours and mine, as men) to be tough, imperturbable, unemotional, in a word borrowed from the Spanish, *macho,* is often one other culprit in the long list of reasons that precede our women leaving. And we don't easily let it go after they're gone.

CHAPTER FIVE

CAPTAIN ROMANCE

T HERE IS A DIFFERENCE between wanting to keep a relationship percolating, as if it were a lifelong first date, and acting as if you are a tough dude on the make. Women are pulled toward the former, repelled by the latter.

One man I worked with told me with pride that he had ". . . made it with a hundred-and-ten women." His supposed reason for coming to see me was that he felt lonely, had no solid relationship, and was ripe for change:

"I go into a bar, check it out, see what I want, and in half an hour she goes home with me." He said this in the context that seducing women was easy but no longer satisfying. Yet, I caught the pride in his voice and pointed it out to him. The bottom line was that he was not yet ready to give up his whimsical sexual pursuits, but when I suggested that, he withdrew and became angry.

After one more session, he broke off counseling. Three weeks passed and I got a letter in which he told me that he knew that he was a "womanizer" and that he was glad I had called him on it, but he guessed he just wasn't ready to change that lifestyle. He signed his letter: "Captain Romance."

When you go into a relationship with unequal expectations—my woman shall be loyal, true, and steadfast, but it doesn't hurt if I play it loose and have a little fun on the side—you are inviting your woman to leave. When you expect your woman to read your mind, automatically know your wants, or when you begin labeling ("You're being a bitch," or, "You're selfish"), you are inviting your woman to leave. When you use one hundred percentiles, such as "You *always* . . . ," or, "You *never* . . . ," this is distortion, and you are risking that your woman will leave. The double standard, whether in the expression of sexuality or of feelings, has gone the way of the Packard, the Studebaker, and the Edsel. And it works both ways. When I asked one man in our first therapy session if he'd been married, he answered, "I was—she wasn't."

Family and marital patterns have indeed changed through the years. Latest figures show that a majority of us no longer practice lifelong monogamy. One out of three marriages now ends in divorce. Among people under thirty, the figures are even higher. Nearly a quarter of all marriages are now remarriages, involving at least one previously married partner.

Yet, these data do not mean that there is necessarily more promiscuity within marriages (or committed relationships). People seem to be practicing what we call "serial monogamy," one exclusive partner for as long as it lasts, then another, also exclusive and again for as long as it lasts.

The number of couples living together but not married has trebled since 1970. Yet in 1950, one out of twenty men and women ages twenty-five to thirty-four said they were "living alone"; by 1980 it was one out of three.

It is clear that romantic, relationship, and family patterns have shifted dramatically. Yet, there is no evidence to show that expectations *within* a relationship have markedly changed. What that implies is that most women (and men, too?) still want and expect fidelity. The difference is that, in the past when an indiscretion was discovered, women were more likely to look the other way. Now, with society more open, women feel more free to leave.

Though my male companions may resent it, rising costs of living began to force more women into the employment market in the 1960s; by now, a second family income has become a necessity rather than a luxury. Many men erroneously conclude that if their women are out there competing and wearing long pants, they are no longer feminine, and the exclusivity commitment has been broken. Women have gained a measure of economic independence, yes, but that does not mean they are ready to abandon fidelity. One has nothing to do with the other.

The case study that follows illustrates this contradiction between the old and the new. The man, Andy, retains the old double standard: his extramarital pursuits ought to have nothing to do with his marriage. If only his wife, Trudy, hadn't found out. . . .

Andy and Trudy:
Dirty Old Men Need Romance Too

Andy is forty-eight, his wife is fifty-two. They had been married twenty-four years when they came to see me. His wife, Trudy, whom I saw only twice, discovered a tell-tale address book in Andy's coat pocket, and, after desperate detective work, found a jewelry box in his garage work-chest filled with memorabilia from different women, some engraved with words of passion and love.

Andy did not deny that he had played around, but begged her to keep the marriage alive. At first she balked and insisted he move out, but her life status, it seemed, felt shaky and, reacting to her loneliness, she agreed to counseling. I presumed they were still living together, but when they met at my office for the two sessions, each time they left alone in separate automobiles.

Then, one afternoon, three days after our second meeting, Andy called and asked for an appointment to see me alone.

Andy: She won't come in no more. She says it don't do no good.

Counselor: Your wife refuses to be in counseling with you.

Andy: I ain't no saint, man. I screwed up. I know it. But what does she expect? She's older 'n me, you know, and she looks it. I can't help it if the younger ones come on to me.

Counselor: The younger women really go for you—and that's not your fault.

Andy: Hell, no. I've been a good husband. We got two grown-up kids. I always worked and brought home the paycheck. She's had it good. I never hit her.

Counselor: You don't see any reason for her to complain about you—about the marriage.

Andy: Nobody's got it perfect. I mean, I messed around with other babes, sure, but you ask her if I ever turned her down. She was always satisfied.

Counselor: She was satisfied but you weren't.

Andy: Well, a man is built different. I never threw it in her face. She's the one who poked around my things, otherwise she wouldn't of known nothing. Then we'd just be going on like it was.

Counselor: So, you're saying if only she hadn't discovered the whole thing, your marriage would be okay.

Andy: Like I say, it ain't perfect. But I don't know nobody who's got it better. (Pause.) Ah, the whole thing will blow over. I know her real well. She ain't gonna keep me out.

Counselor: *Keep* you out?

Andy: Well . . . I've been staying at my brother's. But she's gonna want me back. (Laughs loudly.) She ain't got nobody else to keep her happy.

Andy is still playing tough, his veneer is firmly in place. He does not yet believe that Trudy will show the resolve to undo the marriage. Disbelief. He may not be a very sympathetic character, but the pain of a breakup can hit the appealing and the unappealing alike.

Andy missed our next session—didn't call, didn't cancel, just failed to show up. Rather than assume some grand pattern of "resistance," I guessed that there must have been no crisis and that he simply saw no reason to get stirred up. About four or five days after his missed appointment, he called in a panic and said he had to see me right away.

Andy: She won't let me back in.

Counselor: Something must have happened, some change, some event.

Andy: Oh man, I told her I would try and be good. I mean *good,* you know, not mess around. And then after work I stopped in for a few beers and this babe was there and she was all over me— and wouldn't you know it, Trudy walks in right then. I tried to tell her, it wasn't me, it was the chick, she was the one who put the move on, but Trudy screamed out—right in front of everybody—that I'm a horse's ass and that she was finished with me.

Counselor: Sounds humiliating, right in front of all those people you know.

Andy: Oh man. I'm in it now all right. Up to my ass in manure. She won't even talk to me on the phone. Oh God. . . .

Counselor: I really do catch how devastating this is for you, how . . . painful.

Andy: I don't see no way to make her pay attention. I . . . I stopped over to the house this afternoon to get some of my stuff and she's gone, and changed the locks. I can't even get into my own house! (Pause.) I think the old lady has flipped out. We had fights before. She'd scream and threaten but she wouldn't do nothing. This time she's really gone off the deep end.

Counselor: Well, it seems as if you can't understand your wife's behavior at all. And meanwhile you're having a really tough time of it. (Here Andy shrugged me off. He looked on the edge of tears and seemed determined not to give in to them.)

Andy: I could make it without her. I could get me a woman easy. (Pause.) She's got two VCRs in there. She's gotta give me one. And the waterbed—she doesn't even like it. She can keep the dog, it's hers anyway. (He stops, looking agonized.) Ah . . . shit!

Counselor: All those things—but that's not really what's important.

Andy: She'll come around. I didn't do nothing so bad.
          She'll see. . . . She'll see.

Andy's disbelief gave way to moments of despair, but he resisted recognizing them. In the same way that a fish in the ocean is not aware of water, Andy, absorbed by who he was and had been, couldn't see his wife's perspective, her resolute abhorrence of his behavior.

After twenty years of establishing a pattern of living, breaking the mold comes hard. Now Andy had to learn to do for himself. The temptation was to focus on his lost comforts, little things like his VCR or the waterbed, but he soon became overwhelmed by his feelings of isolation. The reality of his aloneness began to settle in.

Four weeks later:

Andy: Screw her. My life ain't over. She ain't the only
          mare in the stable. (Pause.) Imagine her telling
          me I can never set foot in *her* house again. How
          fast it became hers and not mine. And she don't
          want to give me the tools from my workshop in
          the garage. Says she needs them to repair
          things. She can't keep my tools, can she?

Counselor: Uh . . . you'd have to work that out with her.
          What I'm aware of is how affronted, how angry
          you've become over the situation.

Andy: You're damn right! I'm not a dog or a goat or
          something. She treats me like dirt.

Counselor: And you're not going to stand for that.

Andy: You got it. I got myself a place now—not a castle
          but an okay pad, near my brother's house. The
          only thing is, I need my stuff and she won't give

it to me. (He stops here as if gauging what is appropriate to reveal. When he continues, it is in a dull, flat voice.) I know it seems fast and maybe a slap in the face to my wife, but I asked this chick, she's twenty-eight, to move in with me.

Counselor: Ah, so you're going to have a young woman live with you—and it sounds as if you're concerned about how that will look to your wife.

Andy: Well, I know what she'll think, that I gotta have a female around, that I can't do for myself. But that's her problem. She's the one who pushed me out. I can do whatever I want now. I'm free. (Pause. Then louder:) I'm free!

Andy moved through what I have come to see as the normal sequence of stages in divorce recovery with startling rapidity. He did not dwell on his own actions in the breakup, nor did he stall in a reminiscing or self-pity mode. That seemed to be his style, even in the marriage—not to be heavy, dramatic, or nostalgic.

He liked to use animal images—an interesting parallel, in my judgment—with his emphasis on the animal aspects of his own life. He was not one to focus on the deep, or the sensitive. Sexual loyalty was not one of his key values. His wife was important to him; it was painful to close off their contact, but he was not about to be alone. It appeared as if a "female," as he put it, was vital to his life, but his criteria for that person were not the usual, loving, loyal, dedicated ones. At first he showed characteristic anger, then immediate adaptation to his new life's requirements.

Though to many his behavior might seem odious and unacceptable, to Andy his life worked, by organizing his own sexual, personal, and environmental needs. Many of us can learn about *taking care of ourselves in a crisis* from his actions.

A follow-up eight months later reported that Andy's live-in female had moved out after four months, but in a few weeks another woman had joined him and was still there. Trudy had filed for divorce and it was due to be final any day. Andy seemed hardly concerned by that news, dwelling instead on the information that his new "babe" and he were going fishing in Mexico over the Fourth of July. He ended our conversation by saying: "Arlene, that's my current squeeze, says I'm a dirty old man. But I told her back, 'What's that got to do with romance?'"

Andy may be an anomaly, but he may also be illustrative of a way of being that can have long-term, painful consequences.

Make no mistake, men. If you hold onto that tough, stoic, old-fashioned, macho attitude, you are gambling on joining that one-in-three who is living alone. You may be forced into a lifestyle of "serial monogamy," where you assume Andy's "Captain Romance" posture. Ask yourself if that is an appealing prospect.

Some of us are taken completely by surprise when our women leave. Other times, such a move is a product of our own insensitivity. We need to be aware of the difference.

I recently saw a greeting card in the Hallmark store under the heading, "Breaking Up?" The inside of the card read:

Now you can put your best foot forward without stepping on his dirty underwear.

CHAPTER SIX

HAVING IT BOTH WAYS

L ET'S TAKE THE SCENARIO of the man who isn't all that
happy in his relationship and decides to seek comfort
with another woman. After a year of double-dealing,
his wife (or partner) asks some penetrating questions and he
is unmasked.

At first he denies, then he fights back. "You know our life
together has gotten sour. We don't even make love any more.
What am I supposed to do? Shine it on? I need someone who
wants to touch me."

His partner, an unassertive but sensitive woman, answers: "We could have talked about it; we could have made
changes. You didn't have to go off with another woman."

She weeps and he is touched. "I didn't mean to hurt you.
I was just frustrated, that's all." He holds her—in what is
probably their most tender moment in years—and assures
her that she will not be abandoned.

Now is when my services are solicited. The woman calls
me and comes in by herself, and a process is set in motion
that will ultimately end their marriage. I have observed that
many men resent therapists and marriage counselors for
precisely the above reason. They blame the counselor for
messing up their women's heads.

In the deep trenches of therapy sessions, a person typically must do heavy introspection. A life that has come to
the pinpoint of crisis cries out for examination. It is rare that

someone who enthusiastically self-examines will *not* grow and become more aware and assertive.

This woman begins the painful task of understanding her own motivations and protections, and most of all, the inadequacies that have kept her trapped in an unfulfilling life relationship. Her man tells her he will not give up his new woman, and he sees no need to end the marriage, as long as the wife agrees that he can also have this freedom. Out of weakness, she acquiesces—having him under those conditions is better than not having him at all—and he now has it both ways.

You're Right—I'm Wrong

Robin Norwood, in *Women Who Love Too Much,* speaks eloquently to the woman who is involved with a man who wants to have it both ways. She says that for such a woman to hold on to such a man, "Almost nothing is too much trouble, takes too much time, or is too expensive. . . ." The woman ends up permitting the man to abuse her emotionally, and it is almost always because of her own insecurity and desperation to retain his affection.

In a relationship where such an uneven give-and-take exists, the only way the underdog partner will rise to equality and dignity is to discover through painful self-examination that she is a valuable and unique and deserving person. Instead of deferring to her partner's supremacy, constantly saying, "you're right," which, stated or not, implies that she is wrong, the underdog begins to take emotional care of herself. This shatters the historical equilibrium in the partnership.

Now the man is stunned by her assertiveness and he sees her as "becoming a bitch." Now he explains (over-solicitously) that if she is going to continue to treat him that way, she has to expect his affections to focus more on someone else.

Then, to his surprise and anger, one day she rises up and in so many words communicates, "I'm right, and you're the one who's wrong." Even more, she doesn't wait for him to threaten her with "the other woman" but instead invites him to leave.

And now he exhibits the fury and the blame: "Your therapist put all that crap into your head. You were fine before that damned shrink got hold of you."

"Fine?" she has the courage to answer him. "So fine that you treated me like a child. So fine that you went out and found someone else. So fine that you kept me in fear and pain as your loyal and giving partner, while you played around joyfully and whimsically with your new lover. Well, that may have been fine for you—and before I was aware, it was fine for me—but it isn't fine anymore. Once I'm aware I can't *not* be aware. You may not like the person I'm becoming, but for me it is like finding myself after being lost, like recovering from a death sentence."

In a baffling turnaround, he now asserts his "true intent." He tells her how he only did what he did to get the spice back into their lives. "I didn't mean—I never meant—for us to lose each other. It was just playing around, you know, a little side fun. She doesn't mean that much to me. You . . . you're not serious about leaving? I mean, you don't really want me to go, do you? If I go, we'll lose each other."

And her response, cool, modulated, an icy winter mountain stream, "*When* you go, we may lose each other, but we'll find ourselves. Then, and maybe only then, can we honestly say, I'm right and you're right; it's just the mix that is wrong."

Did I Blow It?

Though I write from a man's perspective, my understanding about women, their motivations and their fears, must be examined. The couple described above first entered my counseling life in an uneven, out-of-balance relationship. In the process of therapy, and in the natural process of resisting what is personally harmful as well, the woman found elements of herself that she had buried away for years. In her newfound strength, she discarded what she viewed as oppressive. Despite her husband's wanderings and confessed disloyalty, when *she* reached that critical point where she would not take it anymore, *he* was caught off guard.

He never thought she would be the one to end the partnership. His experience of her and their history together portrayed her as dependent and childish. This was not the woman he knew. This was a monster created, in part, by the process of therapy, by stirring up stuff that, in his opinion, was better left alone.

There is a tendency to see this new, strong, assertive woman as inhuman, unflappable, a tower of immovable hardness, an inflexible Amazon, a metallic, unreachable Wonder Woman. Nothing could be further from the truth.

When a woman leaves a man, despite her arrogant (and necessary) outer shell, she dies a thousand deaths inside. Every day in every way her new, alone, self-reliant routine bombards her with problems, chides her with remorse. A hundred times she will ask herself, "Did I blow it?"

Journalist Abigail Trafford, in her book, *Crazy Time*, calls this the stage of *ambivalence*. What if your partner changes? "He seems much more mellow now." "We met for lunch to discuss finances and he was so nice."

The logistics of breaking free—the heavy load of responsibility—can overwhelm a woman. Handling all the household duties, paying all the bills, if she has children, the daunting prospect of rearing them primarily alone, the legal pettiness, creating a new social life, earning her own income—juggling all this alone shakes a woman's most focused resolve.

Add to that the history between the splitting partners, the memories (we tend to remember only the good times and block out the bad), nostalgia, holidays, birthdays, moments of passage, children starting school, performances, the first step, the first word, birth, death. It would indeed take a Wonder Woman to ignore all of the above and walk out of a relationship with impunity.

So the woman asks, did I blow it? She vacillates, proud that she had the courage and strength to break free, but uncertain about her choice and the prospect of being alone and struggling. It is precisely at this point that she may entertain the thought of her own version of having it both ways.

Her relationship could no longer be tolerated the way it was. But she thinks, after all, there were some good things about him. We've shared so much. Maybe he'll learn from all of this. Maybe the shock has knocked some sense into him. Besides, it's scary to be alone.

So she says yes to a date for dinner with him. In the back of her mind is the thought: keep your independence and see what happens. But in her heart is the pull to try to reconnect with him and see what happens. Having it both ways requires not burning bridges, while opening up to new opportunities. The sad and mixed message to the man is: I'm not completely through with you; spending some time with you still suits my purposes, for now, but my options are open in case I find myself drawn toward someone new.

The dilemma for the man involves his developing need to

hold onto the familiar in the face of her quixotic attention, her indifference, and the implicit threat of her final departure. In effect, the tables have turned. When a woman asks herself, "did I blow it?" she is struggling to minimize her losses, and the man must then deal with the reality of whatever choices she might decide to make.

Please Hear What I'm Not Saying: Contradictory Messages

Having it both ways also involves the agony of "corrupt communication." At the fragile time of first separation that precedes final dissolution, the language you use can give opposite meanings, and sends contradictory messages, even during the supposed tranquil times. The key to comprehending a partner's message is a clear awareness of intent, which sometimes means ignoring the words and focusing more on the inflection, tone, manner, and body language.

One often-camouflaged intent is *ridicule,* name-calling, buried in an innocent sounding sentence. "Yeah, I know I had an affair, but you don't have to be a cry-baby about it," or, "It's not your playing around that finally got to me, it's your stupid attitude." Cry-baby and stupid (and hundreds of other words) have lots of negative connotations and can instantly trigger defensiveness, a shaky self-image, and verbal retaliation. Such labeling can be lastingly disabling.

Another masked intent which must be deciphered is *sarcasm.* In the middle of a spirited discussion, one partner blurts out, "Of course, you're perfect, aren't you?" Or the other partner might say, "You'd have no problems at all if they only let you run the world." Such cutting phrases divert attention from the real issues, cause a closing off from the respondent, especially during moments of stress, and imply,

"I'm not genuinely interested in discussing things with you."

Moralizing is another message with contradictory impact. "Do what you want but you're going to have to live with yourself," is an attempt to create feelings of guilt, but it is vague and unsettling because it is couched in double meaning. The consequence of such tacit preaching is a digging-in by the other, in defense of her/his position.

Analyzing, though popular and sometimes necessary in problem-solving, is threatening when applied during conflict. A seemingly caring comment such as "You're just tired, that's all," or, "I understand, you're confused right now," can cause "analysis paralysis." The recipient of such phrasing feels diagnosed and exposed. And worse, if the analysis is wrong, the partner can be immobilized for fear of distortion and entrapment. A statement such as "you don't really mean that," can trigger doubt and loss of confidence.

The intent of *blaming* often elicits either an acceptance of the judgment—"I guess I am at fault—I'm rotten"—or an inappropriate retaliation—"What makes you think you're so wonderful?" Blaming sends a denigrating implication of incompetency, fault, even stupidity. It stimulates a counter-attack of blaming from the partner. The residue of blame is a deep and long-lasting pool of resentment.

Even such seemingly straightforward intent as *persuading* can hold hidden, negative meanings. In time of friction there is a strong pull to use logic on your partner. (Men seem more disposed to this than women.) "Let me explain why you're wrong," or, "If you want to know the truth," are phrases which can stir the listener to turn off. Persuasion can be a clean attempt to state a point of view, or it can be coated with subtle criticism. The criticism comes when the covert message is, ". . . how can you be so thick?" Even an innocuous "Yes, but . . ." when used to discredit a statement, delivers mixed intent.

An obvious threat, often disguised as, "This is for your own good," is the intent to send out a *warning*. "If you do move out, you'll be sorry," or, "Remember, there's no turning back." These are verbal attempts to burn your partner's bridges. It often produces a temporary fear or submissiveness which later turns to anger, or it could promote an "I'll show you" reaction to test the threat. Warning often backfires by initiating rebellion.

Reassuring is what well-meaning friends and relatives often do. Even then it can send a mixed message, but when the estranged partner begins to reassure, it virtually assures the other that he/she is being misunderstood. "Don't worry, I'll always love you," might really mean, "I'm getting ready to leave despite feelings of love." Or, "Everything will be all right," could really mean, "Even when we break up, the world won't end." In these cases, the underlying message dismisses the partner's deeper feelings. She is worried. He does feel miserable. To say "don't worry" says "don't feel the way you do." An impossible piece of advice—and insulting.

Dr. Thomas Gordon, who several years ago did some excellent work on Parent Effectiveness Training, has used some of the above distortions (and others) to illustrate ways that communication can become ineffective and damaging. The benefits of learning effective communication skills include less power struggles and verbal punishment, allowing for warmer and closer relationships to develop.

I consider contradictory messages to be masked attempts to slap out at an alienated partner, to punish, while using camouflaged, controlling language. They are attempts to have it both ways. Yet, if you can believe in the natural drive by people toward healthy behavior, they may also be heard as a hidden plea: please hear what I'm *not* saying.

Just Friends, Lovers No More

What I'd like to be able to say to my alienated partner is: "Look, I'm hurt too. No one is to blame. Both of us forgot to be attentive. We let it go too far, let it get away from us. We stopped being lovers, and it's put a strain on our friendship too. Even a friendship withers without loving allowances. We may not be able to recapture the love we squandered, but perhaps we can regenerate our friendship."

With almost every love that fails, there is the unshakable hope that an abiding friendship will remain. One woman client of mine, even as she chose to go to another man, said to her partner, "I can't imagine my life without you in it." Yet for the next three years she had no contact with him. Then, when the new relationship sputtered, she contacted him again. This time their connection reached a pleasant level of friendship, but no more. The passion had, as they say, cooled.

Why this relentless, almost desperate need among us to stay connected to a person who may have, in one form or another, told us to get lost? Is there an internal masochistic streak that we all, unknowingly, carry around? Is it one other way that each partner, the leaver and the left, seeks to have it both ways?

Daniel Levinson, in his important book, *The Seasons of a Man's Life* (the informational basis for the best-selling book *Passages*), talks about a midlife transition at the age of forty, a time of awareness for all of us, whether or not one has succeeded in "becoming his own man." Some men, in appraising their lives up to this so-called midpoint, decide that significant changes are needed. One of these changes might involve divorce, remarriage, or renegotiating a relationship. This is how one *individuates* at a key, crisis point in life, or, said another way, how one forms a new sense of who he is, to define the boundaries between self and world.

Others have postulated a similar crisis point for women, sometimes called the "empty nest syndrome" when children are involved, but in recent times more likely an identity and boundary crisis not unlike the man's. *Who the hell am I?* a woman asks herself. Is this how I want to live out my life? And in a partnership where she has felt unappreciated, her answers foment revolt.

Men and women both face these adult identity crises with an influential history; they cannot consider any changes at this point unencumbered, free, or without emotional baggage. This baggage keeps the change from being clean; we are tempted by it, to hold onto the familiar, to retain what we can from our pasts. Because we do not easily burn our bridges and let go, it appears as if we are attempting to have it both ways—and indeed we try. If we can no longer be in a love relationship with our historical partner, at least we can be friends.

How well does that work?

For one man, Steve, it worked fine, for another, Lennie, not at all. Steve and his woman, Tina, never married but were together for two years. She had a St. Bernard dog that became a focal point of friction between them. While it is unlikely that the dog was the only reason the relationship cooled, Steve pointed to the animal as one irritant that drove him away.

I saw the two, Tina and Steve, for eight sessions together, and one each separately. It became clear to me that he wanted to end the romance—but as soon as Tina began to accept that as inevitable, Steve began to hedge. The loss loomed as a sentence to loneliness, and he scrambled about looking for a way to be emotionally free yet not physically alone. To my mild surprise, Tina went along with Steve's plan to date her every week "as a friend." This continued for three months.

They stayed friends, even after Tina married and Steve had a steady girlfriend. In fact, Tina and her husband intermittently invited Steve and his new woman over for dinner or to join them to watch television.

As for Lennie, his was a more typical scenario. His nine-year marriage fizzled and his wife, Adrienne, asked him to move out. There were no children, and Adrienne demanded a total break: "Just leave me alone, that's all. I don't want to see you again. Ever."

The sequence of events that led up to that pronouncement is complex—and as I mentioned in an earlier chapter, blame is usually a blur. When Lennie pleaded for contact: "It doesn't have to be so final. We could certainly stay friends. Who knows what would happen?" Adrienne answered unequivocally: "I have no interest in being your friend. Our relationship failed. We don't get along. Why should I be friends with someone I'm constantly fighting with?"

From the day Lennie moved out, he saw Adrienne only three times, and those were accidents, running into her inadvertently when he was moving his personal belongings. When their marriage ended, their friendship ended, too.

And usually the attempt to have it both ways is futile. We often, understandably, struggle to retain a closeness with the familiar, what we know, rather than cut the ties and leap into a new, scary unknown. But that retention, more than likely, is not going to last.

Let us assume that we now have a partnership that is beyond saving. There were too many feuds, communication lost, roadsigns ignored. One partner has made her Declaration of Separateness. Now what? How does the left partner—how do *you* and your children, if any, cope?

In my research I have found ample material available to assist a woman who is about to become unattached: how to manage her finances, get a lawyer, take care of her home alone, learn to date again, find a new partner. I found virtually nothing, however, to help a man.

This is all important information for men, too, and we need to focus on what a man experiences when his relationship dissolves; how he weaves through several tortuous phases, grasping for common ground, gradually landing, at last, hopefully, on his feet in a new life scene.

The woman may have already had one, two, three years or more of building up to that sabre-point moment when she says to her partner, "I have no feelings for you anymore; I don't love you anymore." He, having ignored the roadsigns, will be caught off guard. From that moment on, the so-called rejected partner goes through very predictable, sequential, developmental stages.

> *When a woman finally makes her stand for freedom, she has already passed through, often silently but nonetheless painfully, the same ugly phases her man will now begin.*

The man will often see himself as the victim and her as the rejector, but she will deny such a simple dichotomy saying she was victim long enough.

Stages, or phases, are never absolute, scientific postulates, there is much individual variation in the order of things and the amount of time any one person spends in each phase. But like Elisabeth Kubler-Ross's steps towards acceptance of death in her book *On Death and Dying*, there are certain universal reactions to the death of any relationship.

PART TWO

AFTER THE BREAK

There comes a time in some relationships when no matter how sincere the attempt to reconcile the differences or how strong the wish to re-create a part of the past once shared, the struggle becomes so painful that nothing else is felt and the world and all its beauty only add to the discomfort by providing cruel contrast.

—DR. DAVID VISCOTT

CHAPTER SEVEN

THE STAGES

D ISBELIEF AND DESPAIR ARE characteristic of the first observable stage after a breakup. A man who is still in love with his partner cannot believe she means it. "It will pass. We've had fights before. I'll give it time and it will slide away (into that same dusty, unexamined place where all our other differences have been shunted). It is inconceivable that she can be so coldly final. The woman is obviously going through a phase."

But this time is different. This time, her cold resolve is unshakable. If she were anything less than frigid, stone-faced, even insulting, she might waver, and find herself still trapped.

Disbelief and Despair

At this point I wish to introduce a couple, Carla and Paul, whose odyssey through their relationship is a composite of yours and mine and everyone else's. They had seven or eight pretty good years, and two or three lousy ones. Carla is the daughter of two attorneys and one of three sisters. Paul is the son of a librarian and a fireman, divorced when he was eleven. He is an only child.

Theirs had been an idyllic romance, with a grand formal wedding and a honeymoon in Mexico. They had two children, Andrea, nine, when they came in to see me, and

Deron, six. Two years before the breakup, Paul's father had told them, "You two could write the book on successful marriages." Six months before the breakup Carla gave Paul an engraved watch for their tenth anniversary: "Paul—Loving You Always—Carla."

Now Paul stood in the driveway of their home, Carla next to him. She has just said the words, "I don't love you anymore, Paul. My feelings have changed."

Raw disbelief is his first reaction, followed by despair.

He appeals to her *logic:* "If you don't think I've been helpful enough to you or the children, how will it be better if I'm gone? All the burdens of the home will fall on you."

And her response, icy and detached: "Too bad you didn't realize that sooner. I'll manage somehow."

He appeals to her loyalty: "How can you throw away what we've built, the home, the memories? You can't replace the kind of closeness we have, the knowing look at a family gathering, the inside jokes we both know. We have history, we have . . . intimacy."

And her response, cutting and final: "We *used* to have that. It's gone. It's been stifled."

Or he appeals to her *fear:* "There's no one out there like me. You're not going to find it so easy. You'll be lonely. You'll be alone."

And her response a boomerang, hard as a punch: "I've been lonely for a long time. Being alone can't be worse than being in a lonely, hurtful relationship."

Disbelief

"How can you say these things to me? You've been saying you love me, up to a few months ago."

"I was confused. It was inertia. In some way I do have love for you."

And so it begins, the mixed messages: "I don't love you; I do *have* love for you; I'm not *in* love with you anymore."

As one man wisely put it: "Ten billion words will now be spoken trying to figure it all out—and in the end the marriage will end."

There is the possibility that Paul, as a part of wishful thinking, will make the erroneous assumption that if she wants to break up, she will just pack her things and leave. Then, like a frigid knife in his heart, the realization pierces through that, though *she* has made the pronouncement, *he* will be the one to leave. He must leave whatever comfort of home and family their union has created. It will be he who must find an apartment, a new living space, alone, through someone else's choice, without his children, in a new life, in a new routine.

Some men raise their colors quickly and rally to counterattack; most are still hopeful that a "trial" separation might save the relationship. So they go quietly, desperately, a trace of uncertainty on *her* part keeping them subdued. But that trace is, in itself, misleading. It is her own insecurity about the awesome stand she has taken; and once he is out of the house she shores up her courage, her energy triples, and she sets about the task of making her single life work.

Despair

During this time, men report that they sleep little; insomnia is constant. Yet, curiously, drowsiness comes at unsuspecting times, driving in the car, sitting at work. Every contact—even the contemplation of contact—with *her* is an emotional storm, enervating, exhausting. Work becomes impossible; distraction is pervasive. There is an actual pain in the pit of the stomach that won't go away. Weight (which perhaps you have been agonizing over losing for years) begins to melt away; food is a bore and an irritation. Talking to yourself is common, arguing your good points, debating *her* unreasonable, entrenched positions.

Many men report yelling in their cars. (My own steering wheel would have many agonizing secrets to tell.) And some report crying themselves to sleep, though they guard this vulnerability from all but their therapist.

The crux of the absurdity of this stage is that the one person in all the world whom you have allowed to know you—to see as much of you as any man permits—now does not want you. You may be widely loved by friends, family, fellow workers, colleagues—but the person to whom you had been the closest, telling your stories to, showing your pain to (as much as a man permits), perhaps only a few months before, is now your adversary, probably your only adversary in the world.

Paul, after arguing that he would come out badly if he moved to some hole-in-the-wall apartment and would not be able to have the children visit comfortably, rented a spacious two-bedroom flat a mile from their home (refusing to sign a lease). He then slid into the next stage of breaking up, one which sometimes comes after weeks of disbelief and despair, sometimes after months. For Paul, the realization that he was now alone hit hard and he began the sad process which I call Clutching at Straws.

Clutching at Straws

This is a pathetic time in any person's life, man or woman. Paul, our example, is shocked, hurt, painfully stuck in self-pity, afraid of the unknown, afraid of the prospect of a new, alone, lonely life. Carla, though she has "shown him the door," for her own shaky reasons has not quite, not completely turned the key against him. Paul keeps a bruised and tender foot in the open crack. In her confusion she sends what turn out to be hurtful, mixed messages—what one man called the "one percent tease." She tells him that she is ninety-nine percent sure it is over. But that one percent keeps him hopeful, desperate, pitiful.

He hangs on her every word, seeking meaning in carelessly uttered phrases. When they talk on the phone about the children and she says: "The children are doing fine; you don't have to worry about them, Honey," he flashes with excitement. (In my own marriage, "Honey" had become a second name. I might as well, during that desperate time, have been called "Football" for all the affection it conveyed.) Or when she says, "I'll talk to you in a couple of days; drive carefully," he twists the routine words into massive personal concern for him. She says "Drive carefully" to the gardener, however.

And finally, in his desperation, when he asks her for her outline of what she would like corrected, she gives him two distinct messages: "I've told you, I don't have the same feelings for you anymore." After his insistence she says, "All right, then, if you want a laundry list of what I find wrong, here it is. You don't show your feelings, you don't *talk* to me; you only want sex, not closeness; you're never around to help with the children; you don't help me vacuum or clean or dust; you drive recklessly and with anger; you rarely do the dishes; you ignore the broken things around the house—and you ignore *me.*"

He, alas, responds to her second message, ignoring the first one. (What else *could* he do?) In his frenzy, he scampers about attempting, as the song goes, to right the unrightable wrongs. And in so doing his failure is assured because her chart of deficiencies are straw men, without substance; even corrected, they would no longer be a factor in altering her stand.

But he, in despondency, chooses to ignore her more penetrating message of: "My feelings have changed," and clutches at straws. He starts ministering to her needs, plying her with presents and (unwanted) attention, coming over on Saturday and fixing the broken garage door. He car-pools for the children, invites her to dinner (extravagant gourmet bistros), calls her from work—in effect, he courts her as if they were new lovers. He is like a puppy dog bringing the bone for a pat on the head.

It backfires horribly.

She is infuriated. He has changed the practical deficiencies, wiping them away as valid reasons for the dissolution; now she must stand exposed, her storehouse of reasons depleted. Now she is forced to deny him on one single reason: "I simply do not love you in the same way anymore." Paul, dejected, says to her, "But what's wrong? I talk to you. I show you my feelings. I help out with the children. What more can I do?"

"Nothing," she tells him with irritation. "There is nothing to do." And then she adds the clincher, "Why don't you just leave me alone. Pick up the children, stay with them when I go to class, do what you have to do for the house, but keep away from me." Then, seeing the total misery on his face, she adds a hurtful, mixed message. "If we don't see each other at all, maybe I'll miss you."

(One man reported that his wife told him, "Go on a trip—go to Mexico or Hawaii or someplace—we have enough money." He went to his sister's in Massachusetts for two weeks but when he returned, he said to me: "She had grown more distant; I think it gave her time to solidify her new friends, to connect with a new man.")

Paul is too insecure to put so much distance between himself and Carla. He hangs close, searching for some doubt, looking for a sign of wavering on her part. At night he takes to driving by the house, *his* house, to make sure she is home, to see if another car—an unfamiliar car—is parked in front. He tries not to be obvious, not to pester, but when he is with them, he quizzes the children about Carla's actions. When he babysits on the night she is in school, he scrutinizes her calendar, forages in her desk, even—he is ashamed to admit this—picking through her wastebasket for evidence of some connection with another man. One of the few truisms in all of human behavior is one that glares out at us like the Northern Lights: *jealousy is fear of loss.*

Depression

Paul's clutching at straws has gotten him nowhere. He had already lost. His marriage had slipped away—and he now slides into the third stage, *depression.* This is the hopeless time. Almost every man or woman I have worked with experiences it.

When he was still clutching, Paul, as a last straw, offered Carla her sexual freedom, an open-type marriage where they could stay together for the children's sake and since they knew each other so well. After all, their routine lives worked rather well.

"If you're not in love with me anymore—if you don't feel close to me sexually—then maybe that's something we can do outside our marriage." He said it with an aching heart, pained by the compromise it represented in his desires. But now the deep realization settles in that she does not need this permission, nor any formal agreement, to be sexually free. She already is; she has already taken her freedom. Internally, her life has been growing steadily away from his. Hopelessness shrouds him. Time becomes a heavy burden. To be with people is a comfort, to be alone, agony.

When Paul was securely married, he reminisced, he positively needed to be alone—to read, think, relax—and he was never lonely. But in the stage of depression, he cannot tolerate being alone. Now, alone means lonely. He seeks out people. He tells his story a thousand times, boring friends, routing acquaintances. He schedules activities unreasonably, just to keep busy. He learns to make do with four hours of sleep—indeed, can hardly sleep at all. Fatigue is a constant companion, yet paradoxically, at night sleep is elusive.

"I used to be able to go to a coffee shop for lunch by myself, to get away and read, or sit and watch people. I loved it. But I can't do that now. I'm feeling too lonely, too sorry for myself. It hurts too much to be alone out there."

At such a time it is easy to clutch your children too hard. Andrea and Deron would come over for a spaghetti dinner, and he would be stiff, cautious. He would question them about school and their activities, and they would answer tersely, annoyed at having to repeat three-day-old events. When he takes them home, he holds them too long, repelling them with his pain and need. Andrea, at nine, pushes him away, invaded, irritated—and he is hurt even more.

(I recall clasping my eleven-year-old daughter in a bear hug out of my own despair, and her squirming reaction with the one, cutting word: "Weird!")

From Paul's damaged perspective, he is dismally alone. He sees his family unit destroyed, his lover and companion undeniably lost, and now his children slipping, slipping away.

Several men I have talked to had, at that time, particular difficulty with their adolescent daughters. From eleven to fourteen seems to be a most critical time, when the father seems to be the main focus of their hostility, regardless of which parent chose the separation. It is easy—and unprofitable—to treat one's children with frustration. Your temper is short; you feel rejected; and it is likely that your children are feeling vulnerable and agitated as well.

I remember saying to Paul: "I hope that you constantly resist the temptation to come down hard on them." My position, especially with Andrea, was that her sullenness and even nastiness might linger for a long time, and the well-intentioned advice of friends to "show her who's boss," or "don't let a kid push you around," could set up a situation where her adolescent years were traumatized by constant friction. There is a narrow line between tolerating her pubescent unpleasantness, and permitting her to be openly insolent. Personal abuse, either verbal or physical, cannot be allowed—yet she has a right to her anger and frustration.

It has also been reported to me by numerous men that, in the throes of depression, their younger child is a balm to them. It appears there is more "unconditional love"among children eight and younger. In Paul's case, his son Deron needed him, and he needed Deron. There were some tense moments in which both Carla and Paul had to straighten out Deron's misconceptions that he had "caused" the breakup. But after these assurances and the establishment of a regular new routine, Deron's initial excitement each time at seeing Paul was the one salutation in an otherwise dismal period.

It is critical at this shaky time that children's loyalties are not challenged by either parent. Therapy or any kind of consultation *must* include the admonition that children need both parents; any attempt by either to win the affection of a child away from the estranged partner can only be damaging (and may well backfire). Children are more hurt by divorce when they lose one of their parents as a result. Adolescents often become unmanageable, rebelling against controls, their schoolwork suffering, their demeanor sharp and trucu-lent. Very young children will likely cling to the remaining parent lest she, too, go away.

People ask me: "For God's sake, how long is this ugly period of depression going to stay with me?"

And my answer, often unsatisfying: "There is no way to know. Some people are depressed for weeks, some for months."

The critical ingredient seems to be a recalcitrant spark that can loosely be described as a "passion for life." With your feelings shaky, your children fragile, your future a question mark, only an inner fire, a spark of inexplicable hope can make the difference.

The human heart, more resilient, more courageous than we might expect, moves eventually to a new stage with the help of another emotion, one which surges up within us when we accept finally that the old love is gone. I call this phase Resentment and Anger.

For Paul it was triggered by Carla announcing to him that she was starting to date.

Resentment and Anger

They were on the phone. Paul had called to check on a rendezvous time with the children. They had gossiped about household responsibilities, the mortgage, a plumbing bill.

"Oh, I've been meaning to tell you, Paul," Carla said to

him matter-of-factly, "some people have been asking me out and I think I'm going to do that."

Now conciliation and timidity are put on the back burner. Now he challenges. He has rights too! Grim mourning is laid to rest. The bell has rung—but it is a new kind of battle, one he has never known before.

Men report to me, once they have mourned sufficiently for the loss of their love, that they develop strong antagonistic, even vindictive urges. Part of it is due to the realization that they are being replaced; in many instances their wives have by now (if not earlier) taken a lover or a boyfriend. The "good old replaceable me" feeling triggers fury. Whether the end of a marriage or a committed relationship, someone else moving in and filling your spot is impossible to accept with grace and kindness.

One man had it analyzed this way: "When my wife told me she was going to date, what it really meant was, 'I've *been* dating and now I'm ready to tell you about it.'"

(Of all the galling episodes in my own marital dissolution, the most intense by far was calling my own (old) home to talk to my children and having the new man answer. I said to him—which now, in a less emotional time, I am not proud of—"You mediocre parasite, put on one of the children!" Of course, he hung up, for which I don't fault him.)

The resentment of this stage often gets deflected onto the new person. The idea that you, with all your history, your ties, the blood connection, your *fathering*, cannot be with your children—and a perfect stranger can, exceeds the limits of justice and believability.

An important distinction, however, is that when one of the partners acquires a new friend who is clearly new— had no previous connection with either one during the marriage—the hostility is considerably less than when the replacement has been waiting in the wings, or worse, was an influence in the breakup.

As with Paul, one can never be sure. When Carla said she was going to date, the new man seemed too comfortable, too settled in, too soon. His son Deron talked about him—going to play miniature golf with him, playing Monopoly—and Paul would be bitterly stung again. Andrea reacted by saying nothing, protecting her mother, as it were, and seeming even more angry at Paul. In his car she would sit as far away as she could, hunched against the door, her face averted. The way Paul saw it, "She acts as if I smell or something."

With the world turning nasty around him, it follows that Paul would turn nasty, too, focusing on the financial settlement. For weeks, months, he has lived with a sense of diminished power. Insecurity has dogged him. One setback after another—from "I don't love you anymore," to "We have to put distance between us," to "I'm starting to see other men"—have flooded his days.

A sense of personal power is the key to an upbeat existence; Paul has seen himself without personal power.

In Part One I presented three valuable generalizations about relationships and breakups. Here is a fourth:

> *Power in any relationship belongs to the*
> *less needy partner.*

In her angry resolve, Carla has been the one in control, while Paul has been desperate and needy. As Carla begins to need again (the financial settlement, practicalities about custody and security), Paul's sense of control is regained. The pendulum swings back and forth.

One couple I worked with illustrated the power issue exquisitely. The man discovered his wife having an affair with a neighborhood shopkeeper, punched the man out, and moved to a singles complex. I saw the couple together and separately for several months. After four weeks apart, the woman, whose affair had ended, proposed that her husband move back in. He, however, had become involved with a woman in his building and responded that many issues needed resolving before he would return. After another two weeks, the wife hooked up with a new man, while the husband's affair fizzled. Now *he* proposed a reconciliation, and her response: "Not yet—I still think there are several differences we need to settle." Power in the relationship swung back and forth, always residing in the partner who needed less from the other.

(I recall in my own situation how insecure and powerless I felt in the earthquake that hit our home, and how that feeling recurred when my wife announced that our marriage had decayed. When it came to finances, however, I had a sense of influence once again.) As for Paul and Carla, the negotiations for dividing the community property and settling the monthly allowances provided a crucible for both power and friction. I will discuss attorneys more in depth in the next section, but for now, let it be said that the involvement of lawyers, while almost always a necessity, solidly creates a clear-cut "me versus you" situation, with adversaries, winners and losers, and *enemies*.

Paul, in his newfound strength, decides to start dating. He will strike back at Carla. He finds a Carla lookalike, younger, with smooth skin and a fashion-model body and brings her along when he picks up the children. The children answer his ring at the door, and he introduces his new friend. Startlingly, dismayingly, Carla is cordial, warm, and wishes them well: "Have a *wonderful* weekend," she tells Paul.

His strategy has backfired. Him having a woman is exactly

what she wants, for now he will leave her alone and get on with his life. It removes, in fact, her responsibility and any guilt she might have accumulated because of the breakup.

One woman told me that her husband was so furious at her reaction to his date that for three years he never allowed her to see another. Even a woman he moved in with—whom the children knew rather well—remained a mystery to his ex-wife. Another woman reported that her husband, during the so-called angry phase, kept threatening to disappear with the children. But then, enigmatically, he would break down and cry and plead with her to "think straight; think about all you are throwing away."

Indeed, the phases of breaking up are not steel-bound cages—we slip back and leap forward, we hurt and we heal, and we hurt again.

Resentment and anger ride the crest of a wave for a time, usually until the financial issues and child custody are settled. Then we filter into a kind of compromise with life, a bargain with what apparently must be.

Resignation and Reality

This is a healing time. There is a reluctant acceptance of the new condition. Your life goes on. You are not yet enthusiastic; you do not yet allow yourself great joy or excitement. You are in an experimental mood or mode.

The famous psychologist, Erik Erikson, proposed certain sequential task-stages for each developmental point in life. The primary task for adolescence is *identity*. A young teenager, long guided and defined by parents, teachers, and grown-ups in varied positions of authority, throws off controls and takes emotional risks in order to be self-defined, to find identity. Then, Erikson tells us, at eighteen or nineteen, with identity relatively settled, the new task that emerges is *intimacy*. One must learn how to create intimate relationships or face a life of isolation. But, Erikson says, the equation always reads: *identity before intimacy*—for how could you give of yourself, openly, in an intimate relationship, if you do not know who you are?

I believe that this same sequence and equation occurs *at any time in life when there is a major crisis*. When there is a death, a loss of a job, the end of a relationship, you must find out who you are all over again in the new life situation. The equation holds: identity before intimacy.

(I had seen myself as father, husband, family man, homeowner, car-pooler, repairman, gardener, nurturer—for a score of years. If someone, a colleague or friend, asked if I would care to go out to dinner when I was married, my answer was always, "I don't know. I'll have to find out what my wife and/or family are doing." I had no idea—in fact never even thought of—what I *wanted* to do. Then, suddenly, starkly, I was alone and had to think only for me! I had to decide what I, a single person, wanted to do. I had to learn *me* all over again, discover my new identity.)

I have observed that the first great flurry of sexual involvement, new romances, quick "intimacies," are not intimacy at all. They are, if such a term can be used, pseudo-intimacies, and in reality, all part of a desperate search for a new identity. Who are you now, as a sexual person, as a person on the town, as a friend, as a lover!

True intimacy cannot be established until the frenetic energy in search of a new identity is finally spent. For Paul, his new life identity was greatly enhanced by two things. The first was meeting a woman who was also in the process of a divorce. They were two damaged ships tossing in a stormy sea, and their relationship did not last, but it was right for the time. The second was his son, Deron, six years old who slept over at Paul's apartment a couple of times a week. Although there was a bedroom for the children, by silent, unspoken agreement, Paul and Deron slept in the same bed, for the emotional healing that comes with touch.

"Many nights," he told me, "I crawl into bed, swallow my loneliness, place my hand on his little bottom, and will myself to sleep with a small measure of contentment."

Then he added sadly, "Some men let their wives do the parenting, but I've always been an involved father. The hardest adjustment is not being there in the morning and evening with my children. They come home from school, perform in a play, sing a solo in the choir, and I won't see them till three days later. Their enthusiasm is spent, their news is outdated; they hardly care to tell me what went on. It is so painful to accept that some few months before, I was their father every day, their nurturer, their protector, and now I am not needed at all on a daily basis."

(In my own case, in this stage, I remember wondering, what if there's another earthquake without me there?)

Many children, at this time, begin to act in ways calculated to bring their parents back together. They turn hostile when any new people are introduced. They are likely to malinger, to show unusual need for both parents. The *reality* part of this stage must slowly be worked through by the children as well.

One woman I had been counseling for nearly a year after her separation told me: "My seven-year-old son finally said to me he didn't care if his Daddy and I patched things up, but that I had to get a man in the house now!"

Another client, a man, told me that he hadn't thought ahead that far, and so was just realizing now, with deep hurt, that the new man would be telling his three-year-old his goodnight stories.

Another said, "My thirteen-year-old daughter hardly talks to me. I haven't done anything wrong to her. She doesn't even know the details of our breakup. Why does she punish me?"

To counteract some of this, there are actions the newly single man or woman can take.

1. Get yourself the best living accommodations you can afford. Rent or even buy a house if you can, for you need a comfortable place for your children to come, if you are to maintain a close relationship with them.
2. Force yourself, right through your sadness, to develop new contacts, new friends, a new support system; you can't go it alone.
3. Surround yourself with people who do care about you, who do love you, and allow yourself to be nurtured, even if that means breaking a long-standing pattern.
4. Experiment socially, and learn the "new you" as rapidly as you can.
5. Take emotional risks—your life is now all yours and much of the sharpest pain is already behind you.
6. Be honest with and arrange definite routines for your children. They need to be able to depend on you, to know you are there.

A friend of mine told me a Japanese expression which seems to fit this stage of *acceptance*. It goes: *shi-ga-ta-ga-nai*. Roughly translated it reads: "It can't be helped." If a person can look at the breakup in that way, it is like giving oneself permission to let go, to get on with living, and to be in love again with life. What is past is forever fixed. It can't be helped.

The legal profession, while in most divorces (and sometimes in long-term, committed relationships as well) is indispensable, can be a frustration as well. The attorney is an advocate and as such tends to facilitate a *versus* situation. This often results in a protracted conflict over custody, housing, and finances. In fairness it must be said that lawyers do not create the conflict; I have heard their argument that dissolving partnerships are always fraught with hostility and their job is to maneuver a settlement in spite of it. So the *feelings* of the protagonists, the man and the woman, are not the major concern of legal counselors.

In recent years, the field of Divorce Mediation has emerged. These trained counselors specialize in the divorce process; they know the laws but work within a therapeutic framework. One mediator I know suggests three meetings, at the end of which a settlement is drawn up and each partner is encouraged to see an attorney once, for editing and legal pruning. Though some attorneys resent such intermediaries, the fact is that it can save huge sums of money and create more amicable dissolutions.

A caution: It cannot work if the partners are unable to communicate, unwilling to compromise.

Many horror stories come to me about the thousands of dollars spent on the divorce, and the process itself, in the end, is unsatisfying, even humiliating.

In my own situation, my wife and I finally settled the finances, told the attorneys the details, and watched as they wrote up the settlement all wrong. Our children's names were wrong, custody was wrongly listed, property issues were omitted. And ultimately—the final insult—when the divorce was completed I was not even told about it. Since I did not contest it, I received, after the fact, a note from my lawyer which read: "Enclosed herein please find a *'Notice of Entry of the Final Dissolution of Marriage.'* Thought you might want a copy for your files." I felt abandoned, a victim of bureaucracy.

Every couple who breaks up or divorces,
should face each other—as they did when
they pledged or married—look each other
in the eye and end their relationship.

For Paul, the stage of Resignation and Reality focused on a satisfactory negotiation for the custody of his children. He wanted to co-parent, a joint custody arrangement in which the children switch residences at standard intervals, but his work schedule and other practicalities (including Carla's resistance) prohibited this. He settled for joint *legal* custody (a say in the important life decisions of the children), and unrestricted contact.

He appreciated his own attorney, but in the heat of one joint session offered, without standing on ceremony, to punch the lights out of Carla's.

"I can't remember anyone I was ever so furious at," he told me, re-creating his agitation.

"Why?" I asked him, tauntingly.

"Because he . . ." he paused, then finished with a touch less vigor, "he kept putting out these absurd arguments to justify Carla's demands."

"Who are you really angry at?" I asked softly.

He thought for a moment, then said with resignation, "Carla."

Rebirth: The First Bounce

The Chinese word for grieving, roughly translated into English, means: "Retelling the story to someone who wants to listen."

Rebirth comes when you feel listened to and understood. There is no predictable timetable. Mourning following a loss establishes its own pace. Recovery is a matter of perspective. Yet, some salutary generalizations can be made about men and women after loss, when they finally claw their way to the garden-gate of *rebirth:*

1. In the process of learning to be open and honest about your feelings of hurt and pain, you have become a more self- disclosing, open person; this infuses new energy and potential into your life that was never there before.
2. Greater motivation exists now than when you were partnered; you may have been sliding along in your life, almost winding down toward middle or older age and retirement; now you find new goals, new interests.
3. You may "see" sunsets for the first time in years, or appreciate music more deeply, or in a philosophical sense, be able to live more fully, in the moment.
4. Greater frankness exists; emotional game-playing comes to seem like child's play; you are more direct and more willing to state openly what you feel.
5. You may even be aware that your partner had more courage than you did—to recognize a decaying condition and break free.
6. If you unburden yourself of bitterness, you may find that you are happier now than you were in your relationship; your nostalgia was for an earlier time, a condition that no longer existed.

The Rebirth time also offers a challenge: that you come either to a point of forgiveness or a point of neutrality with your ex.

When the child custody arrangements are such that ongoing contact is inevitable, at least a working amicability must be reached. Joint custody, any form of mutually shared, physical custody, requires a genuine harmony between the adults.

Some people report becoming close friends again with their ex-partners. Some talk of being occasional lovers with their ex-partners. In a few cases, bitterness and resentment linger for years, most often where the children are concerned.

One man, three years after his divorce, told me: "Now I'll open a bottle of wine, pour it gently and savor its bouquet and color, whereas a few years ago, enmeshed in an unexamined routine, I would have swallowed it in a single gulp."

Paul said to me, at last, when his passion had settled and his new routine was in place: "I've gone dancing. I ate escargot. I went out on a sailboat—first time in my life. I can't believe the new things I'm experiencing."

The new things he was experiencing used to be labeled, "going through a second adolescence." But it can be seen as coming alive again. This phase is marked by a more carefree, experimental attitude, and a surprising capacity to feel alive in the present.

Though I do not advocate a traumatic divorce as the best way to get to a place of full functioning in the moment, there is no doubt that the heavy focus on life processes and self often precipitates such an outcome. (More on this in Chapter Nine.)

The well-known pianist-comedian, Oscar Levant, once wrote: "The trouble with most Americans is that happiness is something we remember, not something we experience." Why is this so? Why do so many of us find joy in memory and not in daily, moment-to- moment living?

Robert Burns, the famous Scottish poet, in his ode, "To a Mouse," (from which John Steinbeck took the title of his book, *Of Mice and Men*), wrote:

Still thou art blest compared wi' me!
The present only toucheth thee:
But oh! I backward cast my e'e
    On Prospects drear!
An' forward tho' I canna see,
    I guess an' fear!

As far in the past as 1785, existential, in-the-moment living was also challenged by old pain and future apprehension.

In one sense we would have it no other way. Humans have that capacity to remember the past and apprehend the future. But if our *feelings* are not in the present, then that present is lost on us. Imagine going to the well-known Scandia Restaurant and ordering their special Beef Copenhagen, and being so absorbed in some past or future stress that the entire meal—and forty dollars—is totally wasted.

The process of relationship dissolution, for most people, is painful and unrelenting. It provides also, if looked at with a "vacuumed" eye, many opportunities to live a full and present-time aware life.

As we move on, new prospects become available as we recover from the loss of a love, and there is much learning to be garnered from the experience.

1. Our ability to be intimate is what life is all about.
2. Saving face may lose us our relationship.
3. Hurt and fear and anger and grief only dissipate when we express them fully, openly.
4. Time is a lovely healer, yet we cannot sit on our hands and expect time alone to heal.
5. Each encounter with another is a unique moment in the universe, and we may flourish only if we treat it that way.
6. The present requires our full attention; remember the past, anticipate the future, but live fully in the present.

If we learn our lessons, we may even have the chance to learn to *love* again—perhaps more profoundly than before. We can experience *intimacy* again—an uplifting state of being, rare and beautiful. And we *will learn to trust* again— a willingness to be transparent and vulnerable—clearly the most difficult attitude to regain.

CHAPTER EIGHT

ILLUSTRATING
THE STAGES

THE STAGES JUST PRESENTED—with Paul and Carla as the primary example—might be looked at as an unusual fit, or an atypical situation. Here is another, different kind of case, but with the same general pattern of stages showing through.

A Weighty Problem

Brad and Karen were married for four years, with no children and no complicated finances except for a house bought in the third year of their marriage. From their first session with me they bickered constantly about chores, responsibilities, bill-paying, shopping, record-keeping, vacations, and almost every other issue which in a partnership required attention.

But another theme seemed to intrude intermittently, and finally leaped out as a major conflict. When they married, both were checkers in a supermarket and both were considerably overweight. Karen had since started her own business doing floral arrangements; Brad became a partner in a funky, youth-oriented coffee house. Karen had lost sixty pounds; Brad had not. That, it became clear, was Karen's issue.

Disbelief and Despair

Karen: I can't help it Brad. It's not so much what you do or don't do. I'm just not attracted to you anymore.

Brad: Big deal. So you went on a diet. Now you think every guy in the world is hot for your bod.

Karen: Don't be ridiculous.

Brad: Well, why else would you be so flip about our relationship? You think you're some kind of beauty queen now. That won't get you happiness. You'll be lucky if it gets you laid.

Karen: You miss the point. It has to do with self-esteem. The fact is, you don't like yourself very much, or else you'd do something about the way you look, too.

Brad: Bullshit! You had no problems with my self-esteem when your adipose tissue amounted to the same as mine.

Karen: Do we have to talk about this? Is this what counseling is supposed to be?

Counselor: Karen, you have a problem with how Brad looks. And Brad, you think that's a phony issue. Yet here we are, with a struggling relationship, lots of bad-mouthing, and no intimacy between you.

Brad: She's too critical, that's all. If she'd ease up a little, we'd work it out.

(Here Brad stops and stares at Karen. There is a long silence and finally Karen breaks it, softly, tentatively, a quiver in her voice.)

Karen: Brad, I'm not sure I want to work it out anymore.

Brad: What does that mean?

Karen: (Pause.) I . . . I want out. (Silence.) I want a divorce.

Brad: You're joking.

Karen: I'm not.

Brad: Our house. Our families.

Karen: I can't help it.

Brad: Can't help what?

Karen: Brad, it doesn't do any good to get angry or nasty.

Brad: I'm not nasty! (said loudly) I'd just like to know what you're talking about.

Karen: I'm . . . talking about our marriage. I haven't been happy for a while now. I think it's clear, our marriage is over.

Brad: (Long pause.) I . . . I don't believe you.

Karen: I'm sorry.

Here is the classic "I don't love you anymore." And it is also the typical disbelief response. The unusual aspect is that it happened in a counseling session. Brad is now about to embark on a painful and terrifying journey. His initial disbelief will become agonizing despair.

Karen, in my judgment, is not far off. Brad's self-image is shaky. In the sessions to come, he will see me alone and I will come to learn that Brad feels trapped in his excess weight. He believes himself to be addicted to food—and the fact that he owns and operates a restaurant does not help. Even before his marriage he had worked around food, a supermarket, and weight had been an issue with Brad since childhood. He had been a fat teenager, unpopular, solitary. Karen insisted, almost cruelly, that he move out of their home at once. (Her determination was predictable; it is the only way that the so-called rejector can stick to her resolve.) Brad protested, procrastinated, and finally after three agonizing weeks, moved to a small room in the rear of his restaurant. After being alone for one week, he came in to see me:

Brad: Karen and I were a match. We fit just right; then she changed.

Counselor: She lost all that weight. It's as if you look at that as a betrayal.

Brad: I don't know about that. I mean, she changed by getting . . . uh, ugly. All of a sudden she couldn't take me as I am.

Counselor: She became critical.

Brad: Exactly. (He stops and his face changes, his voice lowers.) Nobody else will want me. I haven't been alone for a long time.

Counselor: Yes, I imagine it's very lonely—and if you think you don't have any prospects . . .

Brad: Who would want me? I've got no energy and I'm not rich or anything. And besides, I'm a butterball. Fat people get stared at but not touched.

Counselor: What a hopeless feeling.

Brad: Yeah. (Pause.) My place is so little, just a hole in the wall. (Long pause.) All my things are still there in the house. I don't see how Karen can stand it, being there, looking at all the stuff we shared. . . . I still don't believe this. I don't believe it. She's got to come around. Maybe if I. . . .

The stage of Disbelief and Despair surrounds Brad, absorbs him. He feels sorry for himself, lonely, unappreciated. And worse, in his low esteem he sees little hope for creating a new relationship, for finding new intimacy. At the end of our session he begins to wonder about Karen's perceptions, the first stirrings of Clutching at Straws, and says, "Maybe if I . . ." but doesn't finish the sentence.

He came in the following week fully into the puppy dog phase, and as seems the pattern, it gets him very little:

Brad: I told Karen on Sunday that I understand now what she's been wanting and that I was ready to give it.

Counselor: And?

Brad: At first she laughed—not ridiculing, just surprised. I said, "Tell me what you'd like me to do. You want me to handle the checkbook, pay the house bills, the mortgage, and the credit cards? I'll do it. You want me to do the shopping, I'll do it. What about vacuuming? You got it."

Counselor: And her reaction?

Brad: She seemed weird, almost crazy. Just started walking slowly around me, circling me, without saying a word. So I said again, "Go ahead, tell me what you'd like done." She stopped suddenly and shuddered like she was cold and I saw this glint in her eye. She pointed her finger at me, cold, hard, a controlled fire, and said bitingly, "Don't you dare try to seduce me like that. I'm telling you for the last time, I don't love you anymore."

Counselor: Sounds so final, so certain.

Brad: Yeah. Now I don't know what to do. I guess it
        really is going to be over. I'm not sure I even
        know how to live all alone. I've been with Karen
        for five-and-a-half years, four of them married.
        (Pause.) I sure wish you could tell me what
        to do.

I'm sure he did. At such a hopeless time, any input, any
guidance at all feels welcome. But no one else could tell
Brad—nor any man or woman going through an uninvited
breakup—what to do. He began to relate his sad story to old
friends, people (he told me) that he hadn't even seen in five
years. His immediate family, a brother and sister and his
mother, became a refuge. His work suffered, though he was
lucky that he had a partner and hard-working employees. He
slid slowly, in oozy, relentless quicksand, into the stage of
Depression. Ten days later I saw him again.

Depression

Brad: I'm sick. I got the flu last week and my body
            still aches. I had a hundred-and-two fever and a
            sore throat. Total misery. (Pause.) The only good
            thing is I lost five pounds.

Counselor: When you're down, everything seems to go
            wrong.

Brad: You said it. Seems like the business is having a
            slump, my so-called friends are all busy or out
            of town, and even the weather sucks. Rain,
            gloom, blustery wind. And on top of it all, I get
            sick.

Counselor: It's like the final humiliation.

Brad: I feel like I want to go away, move out of town, start over, or something.

Counselor: I hope you'll think twice about making any serious life decisions when things seem so desolate.

Brad: Oh, I know. I'm not going to jump off a building or anything. (He pauses here then tries to make a joke on himself—which I found to be a twisted denigration.) I'd probably land on a car and crush it in—and bounce.

Counselor: So critical of yourself.

Brad: Well. Look at me. I've got the body of a rhino.

Counselor: And the heart of . . . ?

Brad: Oh, the heart. I've got a heart all right. A broken one. No, a smashed one. No prospects, nothing. I'm trapped in this huge balloon they call a body that only a mother, or another trapped balloon, could love. My partner balloon let the air out and whooshed away, and here I am the only balloon left in town. (Pause.) . . . Shit!

Counselor: Everything you think about yourself right now revolves around your body, how you look.

Brad: What else can I do? You probably never had to live every minute of your life thinking that people are staring at you, wondering how you fit in a theater seat or an airplane, or how you tie your shoes. I've been fat, a fat *slob* since I was ten years old!

Counselor: That's how you *have* been. And it sounds as if you're resigned to being that way from now on, too.

Brad: It's hopeless, hopeless.

Counselor: That's . . . how you feel. There's nothing you can do about it.

Brad: I *can* do something . . . but I don't. (Pause.) I mean . . . I haven't.

Counselor: It comes down to taking a risk, breaking a pattern.

Brad: What good would it do? I'm kind of a pathetic character, don't you think? A joke. That's it, nature's joke. Even my wife finally caught on. Look at me, good for a hearty belly-laugh, that's what I am.

Counselor: If you think you're a joke—that people laugh at you—what do you want to do about it?

Brad: You know, they don't laugh at me once they get to know me.

Counselor: Once they get by the first, superficial physical impression.

Brad: That's right. I guess I'm a nice enough person.

Counselor: Yes. It sounds as if once *you* get past the superficial physical impression, you think of *yourself* in a pretty good light.

Brad: (Pause.) Yes. Yes, I guess so.

This is a typical session when a person is deep into the Depression stage. Self-deprecation is universal; the feeling ". . . if she doesn't want me, she who knows me most profoundly, then I must be unlovable, a pitiful, hateful person." To compound the usual low self-image is Brad's horrible sense of his physical presentation; he can't stand how he looks and that colors all aspects of his alone and deeply lonely life.

At the very end of this session he showed what I have come to understand as the valiant and irrepressible urgings of the human heart toward its own healthiest state. He said that people who get to know him appreciate him. He recognizes a basically sound *core* self despite his unacceptable *corpus*. At some level he knows that he is a "nice enough person."

My work with Brad from this time on became an exercise in self-acceptance. Could he live an acceptable and even enjoyable life in a body he considered to be unappealing, especially in the after-glow of rejection by Karen? Ideally, he would begin to lose weight, regain a sense of vibrancy, find a new relationship, and start life over; but more likely, he would have to learn to live contentedly despite the way he looks—he has already looked like this for the majority of his years.

Psychologist Carl Rogers maintained that the primary challenge of every human life is self-understanding and self-acceptance. He believed that no one could understand or accept himself as he was until *another* has first understood and accepted him. Feeling thus understood and prized, he then gains permission to prize himself.

My aim with Brad was for him to prize himself as a unique and marvelous human being. Two months passed. I watched as Brad seemed to bottom out, and the first sparks of anger erupted. In one of our meetings he verbalized rather eloquently his newfound energy:

Resentment and Anger

Brad: Everybody deserves love. Even fat people. Karen didn't understand that. She didn't understand me. She thought my body, my rounded, rolled, nonathletic, nonstreamlined body was me. How wrong she was. Damn, was she wrong! (Long pause.) I once lost sixty pounds in five months. Then in the next six months I gained back forty-five. It was a roller coaster. (Pause.) My weight seems to be glued to my mood. When I'm cruising in my life I seem to forget about it, fat, slim, what does it matter? But when I have a crisis I either panic and start to eat like crazy or I swear to myself to go on a diet. (Pause.) Life's a circus, you know?

Counselor: That sounds like a question.

Brad: Well, it is a circus sometimes, some weeks. Then other weeks it settles into a routine, smooth, un-spectacular, even dull. (Pause.) This past week I went over to the house and hauled away a lot of my stuff. Karen watched me to make sure I didn't take her records or books. Pissed me off.

Counselor: So, what did you say?

Brad: I told her to buzz off. I could take whatever I wanted—even if that isn't exactly fair, it's how I felt.

Counselor: Lots of anger coming out.

Brad: To hell with her! She's the one who's screwed up, not me. It's her values that are distorted. (He laughs.) I saw a poster that had one-liners all over it: "I may be white, I may be black, I may be fat, I may be skinny, I may be Jewish, I may be Mexican." Then, in the middle of it all, in big, red letters it said, "Love Me, I'm a Human Being."

Counselor: You seem like you're really tuning in to other things, other aspects of yourself than weight.

Brad: Karen's the loser. She . . . loses *me*.

I felt like applauding. There was an extended silence, during which I could see a kind of pleasure on Brad's face. It seemed to be an important moment, a moment of insight, to be savored, not to be interrupted. Finally, Brad said:

Brad: I'm going to make it. It's hard, but I'm a strong person. I still love Karen, probably always will, but our close relationship is history. Maybe we could become friends again some day, but for now I need to push her out of my thoughts, get on with my life.

And so the Anger stage is felt and gives way, sometimes after weeks of it, sometimes in a single moment of revelation, to a kind of compromise with life. It is "it can't be helped" time, recognition that fault or blame are elusive concepts and only the reality of life can be tangibly addressed. Brad's "problems" do not go away. He will discover that they will continue to surface for consideration because life is not crisis-free. The counselor hopes that Brad will have obtained the tools to handle the inevitable crises that will certainly come up.

It was three months later, about eight months after Karen's declaration of dissolution, when I saw evidence of the new plateau Brad had reached.

Brad: I've been stuck. You know, not able to see things clearly. Karen hurt me a lot—well, she did what she did and *it* hurt me a lot. I'm not

blaming her. She went for something better, as
she saw it.

Counselor: So you're beginning to look at it differently,
beginning to think of Karen as struggling to better herself.

Brad: It's easy to be a victim forever. (Pause.) I met
someone who seems to like me. We haven't had
sex or anything. I'm not even sure we will. But
she laughs with me and we've gone to the movies a couple of times. (He laughs.) She's a skinny
thing, but you know she doesn't seem to pay
any attention to my weight.

Counselor: A good friend who looks beyond the physical.

Brad: Well, maybe not completely. Maybe she doesn't
care that much about sex. I don't know yet.
(Pause.) What the hell, even if she doesn't work
out as an intimate person in my life, I'm having
fun with her, and she is with me too, I think.

Counselor: You seem *up* to me, and at the risk of a bad
pun, lighter—uh, in spirit.

Brad: (Laughs again.) Yeah. I feel lighter, and I'll tell
you a little secret. With fat people it's hard to
notice, but I've lost twelve pounds.

Counselor: Hm. What's behind that?

Brad: I'm not sure. It might have to do with my new
friend. Or it could be the new energy I've been
feeling. I've been thinking there are lots of
things I want to get done in my life. I enrolled in
a photography class that starts next week. My
partner and I have been talking about opening a
second cafe, over near the university.

Counselor: New projects, new goals, a kind of rebirth.

Brad: That's it! I even see more things now, little
things that used to be cloudy or hazy. Like
flowers or the wind blowing or children playing.
Here, see this. (He produced a crinkled paper
that looked as if it had been frequently folded
and unfolded.) I found this quote by George
Bernard Shaw. It seemed like it fit me pretty
well: "The only true joy in life is being used for
a purpose recognized by yourself as a mighty
one: being thoroughly worn out before you are
thrown on the scrap heap; being a force of
nature instead of a feverish little clod of ail-
ments and grievances complaining that the
world will not devote itself to making you
happy."

He read it to me with an eerie fervor that I saw as poignant, and almost spiritual. Brad had found something himself, a new way of looking at life, as an opportunity rather
than punishment, a challenge rather than an obstacle.

I used the word rebirth with him, not in a religious sense
but meaning renewal; a recovery of some of the zest and
spontaneity we all came in with at birth.

He saw me three more times, skipped a month, then saw
me once more. Though he never mentioned it to me again, I
thought he looked slimmer—his movements crisper, his
manner more energetic. In that final session he told me that
Karen was getting married and that it bothered him but not
in a debilitating way. He had, he said, enough stimulating
activities in his life that he didn't dwell on Karen and her
"crazy" choices. There was clearly and understandably a
spear of disdain in his words.

As is often the case, I lost track of Brad for a year and a half. In such instances I presume my client is doing well, substantiating the saying "no news is good news." When he called me again he made an appointment to, as he put it, check in and catch me up on things. My presumption proved accurate. He was feeling well, had been studying photography and doing some free-lance work. His partner and he had gone ahead with the second cafe and it was flourishing.

Finally, he told me, Karen was getting another divorce. He said it with no trace of satisfaction as far as I could tell. Then he added philosophically, a remote look on his face, "Change seems to be her style. Moving on to new things. Maybe that's just who she is."

When he left me that day I thought to myself, you've come a long way, baby. I was particularly struck by the fact that in that entire hour he never once mentioned his weight.

PART THREE

BOUNCING BACK!

*Someday, after we have mastered the winds, the
waves, the tides and gravity, we shall harness . . . the
energies of love. Then for the second time in the history of the world man will have discovered fire.*

—TEILHARD DE CHARDIN

CHAPTER NINE

SUPPORT GROUPS

WHEN LOVE WITHERS there is, of course, a sick feeling, and legitimate sadness ensues. But in a practical sense, there is a new gaping hole in your life. If it is your marriage that ends, your entire routine is altered: where you live, where you eat, where you sleep, your neighbors change, your companions are different. If an unmarried but committed relationship ends, your weekends and evenings are dramatically changed. A vacuum exists now, which you have to fill, unscheduled hours, and social events at which you are now unwelcome. One client, at the dissolution point of a two-year relationship told me: "I know she's in misery and so am I. After we had our moment of truth, I felt this sinking inside. I didn't sleep at all. I haven't eaten a thing. My head keeps spinning. I keep wondering what I did wrong."

It is vital to permit yourself to be nurtured; for many independent people this is a difficult concession. Following a breakup, the most powerful feeling is one of emptiness, a lowering of energy in your day. This is a primary reason why so many men and women leap into new family situations or new relationships so quickly after a breakup.

In the difficult process of bouncing back from loss, the most reliable nurturers will be family members, whether the loss is a ten-year marriage or a sixteen-month commitment.

One divorced man had an eight-year-old daughter about

whom he told this anecdote: "Her mother, my ex, just after our divorce, had a new man move in, and he lived there for three years. Now he was leaving. My daughter confronted me: 'Did you know about this?' 'No,' I answered, 'only half an hour before you did.' 'Well, I'm mad,' she told me. Then she stopped and thought for a moment. 'You know, Dad, when I was in kindergarten we used to paint pictures with glue and then dust them with glitter. Then we'd turn them over and shake. The glitter that falls off—that's like all these people that come and go in your life. The glitter that sticks— that's family, like you and Mom.' "

Profound metaphor for an eight-year-old. Can children be nurturers? Absolutely!

Family

Another client, Howard, divorced after a twelve-year marriage, learned rather quickly which activities worked the smoothest when he had his two children. They liked the park —hiking on trails, playing ball; his son went wild on the swings, his daughter on gymnastics equipment, bars, ropes, ladders. Howard sat through many a Disney movie, and the weekly rituals of situation comedies on television.

At night before he tucked his children in bed, he would dutifully (but with genuine passion) read to them, and then make a point of saying, "I love you." And on occasion he would get a return, "I love you too, Daddy." After a time, he could feel nurtured from the activity alone, with or without the children verbalizing their affection.

One woman he dated had two sons, but Howard felt distant from them. That distance, in fact, scuttled his relationship with their mother. (Step-parenting is a special skill which I will address at a later point.)

One gratifying activity turned out to be travel. Since Howard's ex-wife lived with the children, she rarely took them on trips, preferring to get away alone with her new friend. Howard filled the gap. The first summer after he left his family home, he took his children on a four-day trip up the coast. And though it would cost him financially, he learned a valuable lesson for future excursions: Ask your older (9–10+) children to bring a friend along when you take a trip.

Howard's son was perfectly content just to hang out with his dad; his daughter was not. With her girlfriend along, Howard's daughter became civil, polite, even amiable. Howard learned more about his daughter's school and routine activities from one breakfast with a friend along than from all the previous weeks alone with just the two of them.

The first winter holiday A.D. (after divorce), Howard rented a mountain cabin in the snow for five days. It turned out to be the most nurturing time he had known since the breakup. His daughter had her best friend along; his son had his father; they all had cozy moments and belly laughs and snow fights and holiday joy.

Holidays. They often create special family problems after breakups. Parents must figure out a rotating schedule: perhaps opposite years for Thanksgiving, Christmas Eve with one parent one year, Christmas Day with the other. Birthdays often involve splitting the day (and two parties!) at first, but later, as a feeling of conciliation grows, joint parties where both parents share the cost can be planned. The first time such a joint party is tried, it is better if any new relationships are not included. That guideline, too, can be modified as time passes and feelings settle. The first holidays can seem narrow and sparse, as if something were missing. And indeed, something is. Planning ahead for trips or vacations which include friends—such as Howard's mountain trip to the snow—can save the mood.

It would be facile to say that by focusing more on your children—and/or if you have them, other family members—you will eliminate dreary days and reroute loneliness. Those hard times will come and go, but a true rebirth, in which your life feels full and expansive again, will involve new life goals and new friends as well.

Friends

A breakup places a friend in an awkward position. Because friends are usually close to both parties, being forced to choose is an odious task, yet allegiances often come down to that. When marriages end the woman usually stays in the home, and neighborhood friends usually stay close to her. When committed partnerships end, friends who double-dated or shared important moments tend to return to their original friend, the partner they knew first.

Complicating the situation is the peculiar phenomenon that men, when they enter into a committed relationship, often give up contact with their old, single friends. It is a generalization, yet more true than not, that women, married or in a long-term relationship, have and keep friends of their own; men in the same circumstances do not.

When a breakup comes, the man often feels isolated, literally "single." One book, by Richard Schickel, on divorce is titled, prophetically, *Singled Out*. In the fundamental sense of the word, newly singled-out women rarely are "single." They have a network of relationships. Newly singled-out men often have no one to turn to.

A man may have little family and virtually no friends, perhaps an old married college pal whom he has been seeing once every six months. He may occasionally go out with a coworker, but he's married and his wife frets about the single man's influence. He may have a couple of sports buddies.

At first, as the man struggles with panic and disbelief, and then with depression, his few male friends lend a sympathetic (if somewhat impatient) ear. Their tendency is to point out how footloose he will be, with perhaps a touch of unenlightened envy in their tones if they are married or in a monogamous relationship.

But then, when the relationship is positively over and he is truly on his own, friends seem busy, their lives crowded, their availability limited. Add to that the frightening prospect of having to date again, to use skills perhaps long unused, and the feeling of isolation seems overwhelming.

In therapy, people will often say to me, "But, how do I meet someone new? I don't like to sit in bars, and I already know everybody at work. It seems like everybody desirable is already paired off."

And my answer, perhaps unsatisfying, certainly an unsavory challenge: "You don't go out looking to meet someone new. You get your life moving instead. If you like the outdoors, join the Sierra Club, go on hikes, get active in ecological causes. If you like to bowl, join a league. If you are political, get involved in a campaign. Dozens of interesting people like the same things you do. You don't go looking for another person. You go looking for yourself."

It is clear to me—and usually before too long to my clients—that they need an entire new support system. And the trauma of that realization is terrible to absorb. It means starting over. It means leaving a life behind. It means few links to the past: the family of origin, old friendships, the children. Socially, when men or women end a partnership, they will go through a massive overhaul.

Counseling sessions during this time are often deep and poignant. The temptation is to affix the label (and be burdened for years by it): *failure.* A new support group who cares can help you to feel accepted and alive again.

Some people do not establish a new system for many months, even years. For some, as in the case of Paul and Carla, that system develops sooner. Not long after his separation, Paul began dating a divorced woman. Though that relationship did not last more than a few months, it exposed him to a variety of activities and people through which he established some vital contacts: a tennis group that played tournaments and held social events every two weeks; an anti-nuclear informational organization, a cause which he embraced and a place where he felt important and valuable. After a time, this involvement created some close friendships.

He was not emotionally available at first; the new contacts were kept distant. He was cordial but guarded. New people were not admitted into his emotional life, and he—as with many of my recovering clients—felt dismay and a kind of hopelessness that his life could ever again know the twin joys of excitement and intimacy. This is typical and understandable. To trust again comes slowly, reluctantly, over time.

As one man prosaically put it, "When the old life is dying, the new is not necessarily ready to be born—there are morbid, interfering symptoms."

But we carry more vitality and more resources than our barren mood could ever presage. Just as we don't give up what was learned in the fifth grade to go into the sixth, we don't give up who we are to become someone new. We add dimensions to ourselves. Like the complex man who moves to the country to simplify his life, and ends up complicating it more by adding the complicated new burden of simplicity, who we are does not go away.

Noted psychologist Abraham Maslow believed that the highest functioning (healthiest) people might have few friends but those they have are deep ones. The "self-actualizing" person doesn't need others in the way that most people do. But people recovering from loss must not be ashamed of needing friends and supporters.

Crisis is a time for introspection, for sharp self-examination, and a time to bounce new thoughts and scary feelings off other people. We can learn a lot about who we are through the way others react to us. It is likely true that a whole life spent exclusively in looking inward is debilitating and represents a chronic kind of narcissism. But self-study in times of crisis is the way we recover our energy, regain our momentum. Once we like ourselves again, introspection gets put into a balanced perspective, and we get on with the business of living, focusing outward again. That is the value of new support systems, of accepting nurturing by your friends: you learn to see yourself anew.

There is also value in talking to a counselor.

Therapy

Quentin came to me with his live-in girlfriend, Gina, for what he hoped would be relationship therapy but instead evolved into breakup counseling, and finally, counseling for recovery from loss. This is a fairly typical pattern. Most couples seek counseling too late.

That Quentin continued in therapy after the split was to his credit; many men do not. I see far more women through the loss process than men. Once it becomes clear the relationship is lost, men seem to tell themselves, "Well, the counseling didn't work; we didn't save the partnership; to hell with it, let her get her head straightened out." But for Quentin, our sessions provided a focal point for the myriad moods and emotions he was experiencing. Therapy is not a replacement for friends, but is (ideally) a valuable addition.

I have found that people struggling through a dissolved relationship often embrace a "something must be wrong with me" stance. They don't see their malaise as a passing sickness or a valid cause for therapy, but more like: "If *she* doesn't love me, I must not be lovable."

It is critical for the counselor to emphasize that, "You, Gina, are okay and you, Quentin, are okay; it is the mix that isn't working." But for the person who hears this message, the facts of life are contradictory. In the final reckoning, a lovable self-concept is restored only by feeling loved again by other people. That is the purpose of counseling. That is the goal of bouncing back.

Abraham Maslow wrote little about relationships and mar-riage and divorce, but I have found that his familiar "Hierar-chy of Needs" provides an excellent model for charting the pro-cess of recovery from loss of a love. Maslow claimed that people are motivated first by the most basic physical needs, then by basic psychological needs, and finally by emerging growth needs. Explained briefly, when one's need for food, shelter, safety, and sex are at least *minimally* satisfied, psychologi-cal needs can then come to the fore. As each successive need is satisfied, the next one emerges. When one feels valuable and valued (has self-esteem), a sense of belonging to something wider and larger than self alone, of being loved and loving, *then* growth needs burgeon, and clamor to be addressed. These include higher order aesthetic needs such as learning to appreciate music, poetry, beautiful scenery, and artistic

expression of all kinds; having intellectual curiosity, searching out the meaning of life, and understanding more about
nature (the need to know about the world). Finally, one
achieves fulfillment of one's own unique potential, living up
to one's promise—self-actualization.

The sequence appears to be predictable: the lower order
needs must be met first and no longer be the priorities before
the higher order needs come into focus.

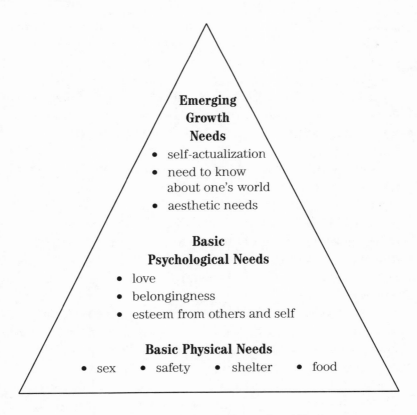

from Abraham Maslow's Hierarchy of Needs

As our adult lives evolve, physical needs and basic psychological needs are usually at least minimally achieved. The final growth needs are more elusive, but some find it possible to reach the point of actualization, living up to our unique potential. This growth concept applies as well to the breakup situation.

Quentin's Growth

Quentin's basic needs for food, shelter, and safety were met; his sexual needs, until the friction with Gina spiraled out of control, were at least minimally met. He had adequate self- esteem and was well respected by others. He felt a sense of belonging at work, at home, and in his community, and felt sufficiently loved and loving. He appreciated aesthetics, loved hiking in the mountains, communing with nature, and was moved by fine music as well; he was a curious, worldly person; he may have been close to his own fulfillment—his self-actualization.

Suddenly he hears "I don't love you anymore" from Gina and the subsequent struggle and disintegration of their relationship sends him tumbling down the ladder. *We fall down to the lowest point, where our basic needs are no longer being met*, and our energy becomes focused primarily at that low level.

I have observed that women in a breakup often settle at the low point of meeting shelter or safety needs, after perceiving their previously secure lives as threatened. There is ample evidence that the standard of living for women falls dramatically when a long-term relationship or marriage ends. Men seem to fall to the level of satisfying their sexual needs, though they are not often clear about this and, for a time, can confuse sex with love, esteem, and belongingness needs.

Quentin's fall was typical in its sexual focus, but he misread his first post-breakup connection as intimacy, hoping and failing to get from it new esteem and love. Our counseling at this time concerned the accuracy of his perceptions, and I raised several critical points.

Counselor: What is your most basic need that feels unmet?

Quentin: I'm lonely.

Counselor: For what?

Quentin: Someone to talk to, someone to hold.
For . . . sex.

If a person has no sexual partner, and is feeling deprived (even subconsciously) by that deficit, to focus on belongingness or some other higher order need may be a misdirection of energy; sexual needs will demand sharper focus, and contaminate pursuit of higher emotional needs.

Counselor: Change can only occur if your desire to risk
becomes stronger than your desire to be safe.
What risks are you willing to take?

Quentin: I'm so hurt that it makes me cautious. I don't
want to be cautious, but if I try to meet people,
to get involved, I could get hurt again.

Counselor: What's the payoff for not risking?

Quentin: Safety. No pain.

Counselor: No pain?

Quentin: Well, not really. There's pain in being isolated too.

Counselor: Awareness and desire are necessary, but not
sufficient factors in recovery from crisis; in the
final analysis, only *action* creates change. What
new action will you take?

Quentin: I'm in a poetry group. That's a risk for me; it
means showing my feelings. And I've gotten
interested in a political campaign. I've already
been exposed to lots of new people, and I've
decided that even when I feel scared I'm going
to speak up anyway. Like, say hello to an interesting person.

I was impressed with Quentin's actions, and told him so.
The risks he was taking were already paying off in making
new contacts with people. Counseling can be a stimulus to
change, but life-crisis therapy does not end merely with
insight. The recovering man must engage in dynamic behavior to satisfy his sexual urges, his need to feel esteemed,
or to belong. The counselor must be aware of the appropriate missing need, and, as with Quentin, help him to focus at
a level that will start him on the exhilarating ascent back
toward full functioning and self-actualization.

That is how one bounces back and learns to trust, and feel
lovable again.

CHAPTER TEN

New Love

"LOVE IS NOT ALL: it is not meat nor drink nor slumber nor a roof against the rain," wrote Edna St. Vincent Millay. Love is not everything; but tell that to a newly single man or woman feeling unloved and unlovable. Then the paradox is wanting and needing love so desperately, but being so unable to trust.

Most first relationships after a breakup are transitional, and end after a few months. A year can go by marked by cautious dating, sexual experimentation, social tentativeness, and emotional turmoil. Then, at an unexpected moment you meet Janet or Tami or Elaine. She too may be recovering from loss of a love. She may be divorced and have children. You begin slowly, mutually guarded, protective of whatever fragile, new, but workable routine you have managed to establish.

She may not want you to stay overnight at first. "Until I make a commitment to a man, I don't want him here in the morning when the children wake up. If the relationship doesn't work, the scene could repeat itself. It's the wrong message to give them." This was from a woman named Elaine who connected with Quentin.

Overcoming Distrust

You may be reluctant to use the words "I love you." But during lovemaking you blurt them out. "It's okay," Elaine says with a soft smile, "I won't hold you to it. Things are said in passion that aren't even remembered later."

"Oh, I remember," Quentin answers her, "It's just that I'm embarrassed. When we're making love, I *feel* as if I love you. Then afterward I get all confused and scared."

The first presents new lovers give each other are usually impersonal or quaint, ideas they catch onto in casual conversation. Quentin gave Elaine a wicker laundry basket with a practical, hinged top. Elaine gave Quentin a towel for the tennis court, imprinted with the words: LOVE IS A PERFECT GAME. They traded off giving each other cans of tennis balls and sweat socks. Quentin eventually gave Elaine a brightly colored and festive pullover sweater, but he was concerned that he didn't know her well enough, might have misread her taste. Elaine gave Quentin a book of poetry but carefully avoided citing the love poems.

Elaine had been a professional dancer, had many contacts and thought nothing of having lunch out with friends, male or female. Though they had no agreement restricting their activities, no stated commitment between them, Quentin looked at some of these dates as potential romances, and saw Elaine as "available and searching." Compounding his distrust was the fact that he wouldn't say anything to her about it, instead resented it in silence.

Connecting and solidifying a relationship with a new person when you are burdened with still-fresh hurts is a tricky and complicated task. It demands skills you may have buried in the painful process of ending your previous relationship, such as showing appreciation, carrying on a social conversation, conquering jealousy, trusting.

The children of a new romance present special problems. Though you may get to know and enjoy your woman's children, you may be reluctant to introduce your children to her.

If she complains about this: "Look, you know my kids, what about me knowing yours?" you may be hard-pressed to explain why, and lamely mutter something about their mother feeling threatened by it. Eventually you realize—and hopefully share this with your new woman—that you don't trust your children's reactions, and worry that they will chase her away.

Perhaps the most penetrating aspect of lack-of-trust is learning to trust you, yourself, again. In counseling, men often complain to me that they aren't sure anymore what criteria to use in evaluating a woman. "I've been stung before. How do I know if I am picking a woman for the wrong reasons? How do I know what the right reasons are?"

The answers, of course, are unique and personal. Learning to trust again means, above all, learning to trust yourself, your perceptions, your own best judgment.

One man, a professional himself in the field of human relations, found that he was having a series of six-month to one-year relationships. He had been divorced for many years and with undaunted optimism would enter into new relationships, all of which, one after another, proved unacceptable. At last he faced the puzzling and punishing reality that he was choosing poorly, for the wrong reasons, to satisfy the wrong needs. It was then that he examined his own judgment and began to consider other criteria.

Helpful models can give people pegs to hold on to. A relationship can always be looked at in terms of compatibility. You might consider whether you and a potential partner mesh in these three general ways.

1. Intellectual.

Are you and your partner intellectually matched? I don't mean IQ scores, but if one person is an abstract thinker and highly intellectual and the other more practical and down-to-earth, communication might be strained. An apocryphal story about Einstein relates that his first wife was also a brilliant scientist, and the two would sit absorbed in their research while the morning toast burned. His second wife, the story goes, knew nothing of his science, but was, in her own way, a brilliant woman, and most compatible with him. Their marriage lasted. Intellectual compatibility does not mean pursuing matching professions; it means being able to connect evenly with each other in thought and expression.

2. Sexual-emotional.

All partners need to be sexually attracted to each other and relish their sexual interactions, but they must also be emotionally attuned. If one partner comes home one night feeling up while the other is down, and the reverse the next night, the two might "miss" each other. Your "pacing" must be agreeable. In my own case—and this is only one example—when my wife and I went shopping in the mall, we would always agree to separate and meet up again in two hours; we knew that our pacing was different, at least in that one aspect, and adjusted to it. Generally, compatibility in the sexual-emotional area is critical if a partnership is to endure.

3. Play.

Here is a small, seemingly simple word that is probably the most important aspect of all. I mean good, old-fashioned, horsing-around play. The kind you do when you are fresh to a relationship, newly in love, and free from contaminating hurts. The play part of relating permeates all the other areas; if you do not keep the play alive, the sexual aspect can become deadly serious: Did he do it right? Did she do it right? Did I get my orgasm? When a couple is new, play can include many forms: walking on the beach, tennis or rac- quetball, theater, Scrabble™, hiking, concerts, watching television, parties, sexual gaming—in the car, in the living room, in the bathroom, anywhere! When the sense of play goes out of a relationship, it can be fatal.

Check yourself out in these three areas. Do you consider these things when choosing a partner? How free do you feel to trust your new romantic interest *and* yourself—particu- larly your ability to choose appropriately?

The Song Is Over
But the Malady Lingers On

Trust is hard to regain because the old loss contains memory-joggers that constantly intrude, obstruct, and obsess.

When I counsel people who seem still immobilized by the loss-trauma, my thrust is toward illuminating the positives of the new life. This demands personally giving permission for the old hurt to recede, and requires what might well be called Promising Points of future light.

Promising Points give hope; they are the elements of life that inspire passion, that get us up and moving in the morn- ing. When you feel desolate and abandoned, it is vital that you establish activities and events to look forward to.

One man told me, "Every day I drive by the little capuc- cino place we always went to. It drags me down, corrupts my whole day."

"What do you look forward to in your day?" I asked him.

He looked at me confused. "I don't—very much. Her mem- ory, it's still so painful."

WHEN WOMEN LEAVE MEN

"It seems as if you feel cornered, like your options for enjoyment are limited," I replied.

"Well," he said, "I can't shake these hurt feelings. It's sick isn't it? Like I'm weak or something."

"I wonder what plans you've made, what activities you've scheduled to anticipate, to . . . enjoy?"

He told me then that planning activities was painful so he avoided doing it. Then he wondered out loud if that might be what kept him feeling lousy. I mentioned the idea of Promising Points and he asked what I meant.

"Like buying season tickets for the Dodgers," I said, "which gives you regular fun dates to anticipate. Or if you like theater, get season tickets to the local reperatory company. If you're a skier, schedule ski trips to the mountains with a ski club at intermittent points. These dates can give you something good to expect, and put juice back in your life."

Promising Points are much like the "future-focus" that counselors give to threatening suicides, events to illuminate future moments, to provide reasons to go on.

Recoverers from loss need continual points of hope in their lives, ongoing expectations that fun and play and joy are possible. These cannot be left to chance; they must be scheduled and planned. A weekend of activities is far more likely to coax out a week of positive feelings than a weekend of isolation and inactivity.

It is obvious and incontrovertible that the end of a relationship does not immediately end all the pain and disruption: the malady lingers on. Only by planning—right through all your shaky feelings—will promising moments be realized. This requires shoring up courage, dancing when you feel leadfooted, jumping in the pool when the water is cold.

Vulnerability and Risk

In order to trust and, finally, to love again, you must be willing to take risks, and this means being vulnerable again.

We all come into the world packaged right, with good attitudes. As tiny children we are curious and wide-eyed. The concept of risk as negative is unknown to us, so we are fully spontaneous and zestful for life. We are adventurous, open, and, of course, vulnerable. So what happens? *We get hurt.* Because of hurt, curiosity eventually turns into caution, spontaneity becomes blocked, and our zest for life slows down. Hurt is a powerful muffler.

When bouncing back from loss, there is a tendency to look at all of living as a risky business. The hapless and often hopeless feelings take the form of harsh self-criticism: "How could I take these risks? I've *never* had the courage to try new things."

Having the courage to risk and be vulnerable is not something you will be learning for the first time; it is something to be regained. In a curious way, recovery from crisis is an affirmation of our childhood; all those risks we took were right.

One's capacity to risk can be enhanced by the unlikely tool of *reminiscing*. It is said of the elderly that reminiscing returns them to an early time of strength and accomplishment. The same can be said of the emotionally wounded. You can, in counseling, work on remembering the energy that made you successful in your job, the charm that interested (and won you) your woman, the passion for life that made you a nurturing father, a nurturing person.

For a time, you may deny your own potential. "I can't" is used often. "I don't know how" is a favorite excuse. "It's not the way I am" becomes the rationalization.

When a person uses these terms, I contradict them, gently

but firmly; the goal is to change the language first, and slowly but steadily change the damaged, guarded perspective. "You haven't known how up to now," I say. "It's not the way you have been acting. But you are not fixed forever in the way you have been most recently. In fact, your immediate past patterns are a clear reaction to hurt. You weren't always that way—and you don't have to be that way now."

A poster in my office will often catch a client's fancy, not at all to my surprise, since it is a powerful yet simple thought. Written by Albert Camus, it reads:

> In the midst of winter
> I finally learned that
> There was in me
> An invincible summer.

Those recovering from loss tend to defer to others: "My father was my protector when I was young. My woman was the strong one in our relationship." It is a huge achievement when a man absorbs the notion of "an invincible summer" within himself. When that concept is really taken in, you are again ready to take on emotional risks.

You can assume personal responsibility for all your relationships again, for the emotional consequences of your behavior. At such a time, the new woman may begin to see the changes in her man and join him in a counseling session. When you are emotionally open and trusting, it benefits her as well. She has been struggling to comprehend all your pain and caution, and wants you whole, available, and emotionally vulnerable. It is only by being open and vulnerable, by taking emotional risks, that the exhilaration of life's mountaintops is reached.

Elaine, speaking of Quentin, told me: "When he said

good-bye to me the other evening, he said with tender spontaneity, 'I love you, Elaine.' I was so moved that I said the same thing to him. His risk-taking encouraged mine. It's the most attractive quality I've seen in him—or in any man.''

A caution: *there is no guarantee against future hurt.* When you are willing to be open and vulnerable, chances are some of your risks will end in disappointment.

Another aspect of Abraham Maslow's ladder of sequential needs, modified to apply to the recovering person, is relevant here. Most of us already function at a modestly healthy level, but when disappointment hits, we become fragile and, in some cases, slip below the hypothetical line of healthy functioning. When crisis occurs and hurt people slide below that line of acceptable emotional behavior, counseling and therapy attempts to help them climb back to being "emotionally okay." But what models of health are being used as examples? Other so-called healthy people, who themselves might be functioning just barely over the line?

Maslow asked the question first, and I repeat it here in the context of bouncing back from loss of a relationship: What are the traits of very healthy people, those who are functioning well beyond the minimal line? In my own language, what are the people doing—and how can I help my recovering clients to reach that place—who have wide margins of good health, who, after a setback, can fall back without having to fall near the line of "emotionally disturbed"?

Put another way, how can my bouncing-back men and women be vulnerable and have disappointments, yet not lose their capacity to function well and return again to even higher risks?

All of us who lose at love need to reach a comfortable place of emotional security, where margins of good health offer an expanded ability to bounce back from all of our hurts and disappointments. Such margins offer a life of renewed hope, with a new kind of freedom.

A New Freedom

The pain when a relationship dissolves may be likened to the pain of the birth process: the product of the latter is a new life, the product of the former is a new life.

The process of breakup and recovery involves intense introspection. Through self-examination comes new freedom from former rigidity, from reliance on old, fusty solutions.

You may be startled to realize that in your old relationship you had become ossified into an unscrutinized routine. Your ways of thinking about a relationship were colored by the hurt and defensiveness and negativity of months or years of sparring with a disenchanted partner. You had begun to look at all relationships as patterned after the only example you knew from the inside: your own troubled, contentious partnership or marriage.

Now, with hard work and steady but delicate progress, you are beginning to see options, alternate ways to *be* in a relationship, that you would not even have been capable of imagining earlier.

An excerpt from the brash and erotic novel, *Fear of Flying* by Erica Jong, fits well at this point of recovery. The heroine, Isadora Wing, tells us:

> I know some good marriages. Second marriages mostly. Marriages where both people have outgrown the bullshit of me-Tarzan, you-Jane and are just trying to get through their days by helping each other, being good to each other, doing the

chores as they come up and not worrying too much about who does what. . . . Maybe marriages are best in middle age. When all the nonsense falls away and you realize you have to love one another because you're going to die anyway.

It may not seem like it when you are caught in the hurt of dissolution, but reaching the place where you recognize that you can easily share all the work and still love each other *will* come. There is a marvelous freedom in such recognition, in no longer being trapped in the old, unworkable patterns.

As a product of rebirth after the loss cycle, we may learn that each instant is a unique moment in the universe, never known before, never to be known again. Pablo Casals, the great cellist, once wrote:

> . . . Do you know what you are? You are a marvel. You are unique. In all the world there is no other . . . like you. And look at your body—what a wonder it is! Your legs, your arms, your cunning fingers, the way you move. You have the capacity for anything. Yes, you are a marvel.

Bouncing back after being left offers a chance for clearer vision, more spontaneous living, and the freedom to interact cleanly, in the present moment, without contaminating historical incumbrances.

Freedom means not only freedom *to*, but freedom *from*. As you move along the recovery trail, you grow more free from toughness, defensiveness, cold, controlling unavailability, and from what has come to be known as the "male macho image." You grow free from the crushing hurts and societal pressure that had robbed you—and every man—of our childhood softness, and tried to turn us into stoics and warriors.

Much study has been done on the concept of androgyny, a way of being that combines our best male and female cultural traits into one. The man, while retaining the positive aspects of his gender, also cultivates the so-called feminine traits of sensitivity, softness, and emotional expressiveness, lost during his early boyhood, what one writer called "the marriage of the sword and the harp."

Philosopher Martin Buber talked about the I-Thou relationship—the capacity to see another freshly, openly, as a special individual, to refrain from objectifying another, making him or her one of a "type." It takes a freedom of spirit to be that way.

I remember stopping a man, gently but with an almost naughty edge in my voice, when he said, "I'm the kind of person who . . . " "There are no kinds of persons," I said, "only unique, one-of-a-kind marvels."

Knowing that you are unique, never seen before, and marvelous gives you an uplifting freedom to be what you truly are now, and to fulfill your promise.

CHAPTER ELEVEN

LESSONS
TO BE LEARNED

I N MY DISCUSSION OF ROADSIGNS in Chapter Three, I cited awareness as the first, indispensable step in change. It might be a cliché to say one should "stop to smell the flowers," but the concept is not. What is there all around us is often ignored. Learning to be aware may be the most profound lesson of a relationship loss. An unattended, unaware relationship will always head for a fall. Often couples will say, too late, "We took each other for granted."

Nineteen of twenty students in a graduate counseling class of mine agreed with the above. Only one woman, in her late forties, said, "Who wants to spend so much energy working on the relationship? That's what's good about being able to count on your husband—you don't have to work at it. It frees you up for other activities." Several of the other students told her that she was lucky that her marriage (of twenty years) had survived despite her neglect.

(It is my hunch that this woman was not so guilty of neglect, that she had likely spent many early years correcting her course, and felt satisfied with where she had come; her dissonance fit her nonconformist personality. Her statement felt to me like a touch of classroom posturing.)

Awareness

Awareness is the *sine qua non* of a relationship counselor's tools. The Gestalt psychologist Fritz Perls believed it to be the *only* right focus for the therapist. Perls' formula read:

Awareness equals present time equals reality.

Sometimes I ask a male client, "What are you aware of right at this instant?" At first, he might respond with a statement such as, "I'm aware that tomorrow I have to see her, to negotiate, and that she will be cold and controlling." He has no capacity to observe and comment on the immediate moment. Slowly, with intermittent setbacks, he might finally begin to see the present, to focus on the *now*: "I'm aware that your shirt is bright red, that I'm smiling, that I use my hands when I talk, and that I'm feeling relaxed."

Though it is something of a game to practice what pops into your awareness, if you do permit yourself a focused devotion to the present, for that amount of time you are not anxious, you are spontaneous, and your response possibilities and life possibilities are instantly multiplied. It becomes a self-training process—with the final goal being higher awareness of all your present-moment feelings.

In an earlier chapter, one man talked about his wife beginning a pattern of dressing and undressing in the bathroom; as the counselor I had asked him how that made him feel. If he could be aware of his present-moment feelings, and act on them, this might have detoured (or even dispelled) the buildup of resentment. Conscious awareness can be applied to all your tastes, desires, personal prejudices, vulnerabilities, hopes, and dreams. Be aware of yourself. Said another way, *know yourself.*

A lovely moment came in a counseling session when Quentin said to me: "Elaine thinks I notice everything. She tells me she's always surprised that I'm aware of her moods, that I comment on what she wears, or that I recognize her tenderness toward her daughters. She's the one who surprises me; I hardly even think about what I tell her."

"What I like," I said back to him, "is that your awareness has become an easy part of you. No, you don't even have to *think* about what you tell her."

Begin to move toward more clear awareness of your personal preferences. Clients have told me many times that they do not trust their own judgment; indeed, that they do not even know what they like and dislike. As trust develops and your willingness to risk returns, your capacity to have and express opinions expands. You will become aware of what you enjoy the most in your lovemaking with your new woman, and will tell her. This openness will encourage her to be open. You will become aware of which foods you really prefer, what form of entertainment you relish most, which music stirs you, and crave quiet moments of treasured meditation.

Most important to your new relationship(s), these forming opinions will be tempered by an evenness in your moods, acceptance born of hard looks at yourself, and will not become rigid, demanding positions. You are becoming patient, accepting, and conciliatory.

"Well," you might say, "I know I don't like Rambo-type movies, and Disney stuff seems childlike, but other than that I'm open. The main thing is to share it—then talk about it afterward."

Your conciliation triggers mutual conciliation in your partner. There is give and take, compromise, and concern for the other's wants. You have become sensitive. You are *mature*, in the truest sense of the word, where " . . . all the nonsense falls away," and competition between partners is seen as a foolish and childish, unproductive pattern.

Expression of Feelings

Along with awareness comes a companion skill: open expression of feelings. Awareness by itself provides new choices, but enrichment occurs only when the best choices are implemented.

Partners will come to me and ask, "Help us to avoid conflict. Conflict kills our intimacy." My response is: "Not true. Failure to resolve conflict kills intimacy." It is not possible to avoid conflict. I have used the image of teens rock-and-roll dancing, where in the entire dance they don't touch each other once—no contact, no conflict. But in a partnership—a love relationship or a marriage—such distance is not possible. And when you dance close, sometimes you're going to step on each other's toes.

The question is not "how do we eliminate conflict," but "what tools do we need to resolve the inevitable conflicts that will arise?" One powerful and indispensable tool is the ability to express your feelings.

In Chapter Two I presented part of a practical definition of *intimacy*. The full definition is:

> The willingness and the capacity to permit your partner to
> see all the way through you—and your partner permitting
> the same—neither of you feeling judged.

If you have created such a state of affairs, in which you have made yourself transparent (and therefore vulnerable), with *one person* in your life, you are fortunate. If you can do this with two others you are blessed, and with three or more it would be remarkable. This condition of being fully known by at least one other person is a vital ingredient in a healthy personality. And, though it makes sense that such self-disclosure be with your lover, it could also happen with a close friend, your child, parent, brother, or sister.

I am delighted when a man reaches a point in recovery where his awareness is translated into action. He becomes willing to be known. He allows himself—not with everyone certainly, but at least with his new love—to be transparent. When you come to this promising point, you will be aware that:

- You do not have to be right all the time.
- You do not always have to be the winner.
- What you "knew" to be true in the past might no longer be so.
- Old solutions might have been the problem.
- Self-disclosure begets more positive than negative results.

QUENTIN'S STORY

One day Quentin came in to see me with a broad, almost foolish smile on his face. "You know," he told me, "my two kids *love* Elaine."

I smiled back at him and decided to hold my comment, to see what else he would say.

"All this time," he continued, "I was afraid to get them together. But this weekend I sat down with the kids and said, 'There's a very special person in my life, and I want you to meet her.' I even told them I was scared because I wasn't sure they'd like each other. You know what my daughter said? 'It's about time.'"

I said to Quentin, "So you took the risk."

His face spread with an even broader grin. "By the time I did, I was pretty sure it would work. So it wasn't much of a risk."

"You said you were afraid."

"Oh man, yes."
"If you were scared then it was a risk."

In a wider sense, what Quentin had been worried about comes under the heading of *step-parenting*. He had read things that had frightened him: 1300 new step-families with children under the age of eighteen are forming every day, and over half of all second marriages end in divorce. He had told me, too, that he had gone to a workshop where the instructor said: "It is unrealistic and impossible to expect that you will love your stepchildren the same as your own children," and, "You cannot assume that since you love your new wife, you will love her children as well, or that they will return your love."

Instant adjustment is one of the major myths of step-parenting. The child-parent bond was there long before the new partner-bond developed. Often a woman will be placed in a situation where she is forced to choose her child over her new relationship. And she will! The antidote to such a crisis is understanding and patience on the part of the new partner.

1. Children are still in the middle-marriage phase while the mother and new stepfather are still in the beginning phase (with all its privacy and sexual implications).
2. You may develop a warm relationship with a stepchild but it may not be a "loving" one, and certainly won't be the same as loving your own, biological child.
3. You are not to be a replacement for the natural parent, but augmentation in a child's life.
4. Allow the child to come to you, and warm to you at his/her own pace.

Quentin had many fears about being a stepfather and also about the myth of the evil stepmother, and it was no surprise that he had been cautious about introducing his children to Elaine. "So what changed?" I asked him.

"I finally realized," he answered, "that there is room for different kinds of relationships in a child's life. I understood that Elaine will not be and doesn't even want to be my children's mother, just as I don't want to be her kids' father. I finally felt sure enough about myself to *say* those things to Elaine, and the release of those feelings—of my worry and my new hope—gave me the freedom to bring us all together."

Prevention Is the Cure

When I was a child, my parents would often invite over members of a social group they belonged to. They would introduce their friends to me—and I would promptly forget their names. It was embarrassing, but they seemed to have many friends who all looked alike, and the names were so similar.

The legacy of those forgotten names haunts me to this day. I often forget people's names the instant after the introduction. Because I am troubled by this, I have tried to understand the process, the emotional sequence I experience that inhibits my relaxed absorption of new people's names.

My childhood discomfort over a task I could not master used to cause an emotional aura to surround that task. Whenever a similar task is presented to me as an adult, my emotions escalate, my old, *hurt* pattern is evoked, and my intelligence—my capacity to bring a unique, appropriate response—is blocked. My pattern takes the form of being self-focused, of being concerned so much about my forgetting that I will not (*can not?*) focus on the other person, on the new name. My thoughts go, "Will I look foolish? Will I be laughed at? What if I have to introduce this person to someone else? Am I frowning? Can I look this new person in the eye?" If my full intelligence (non-hurt awareness) were operating, my thoughts might be, "Interesting new person. I'm curious and interested. I like her hair. I like his shirt." And I might feel free to say, "Your name, it's unusual. Does it have special meaning?" or even, "What a great smile you have!"

Our individual childhood hurts leave us with adult patterns of hurt behavior which prohibit our intelligence from functioning fully. Our adult hurts—divorce or the dissolution of a love relationship—leave us with hurt patterns of behavior as well.

When we are operating out of hurt, our responses do not come from our free, full intelligence but from a protective pattern, rigid, predictable, and self-perpetuating. The process of breaking some of those patterns is the process we have been discussing.

We cannot be completely protected from hurtful situations, but we can learn how to neutralize them so that we prevent settling in to long-term, negative patterns. Those contaminate a relationship, and lead ultimately to the destruction of a love partnership.

If, in my childhood, I had been given the opportunity to express my feelings of frustration and confusion over introductions, my long-term, negative pattern might have been avoided. Such expression might have taken several natural forms: talking and explaining heatedly, crying from hurt, raging with anger, shivering with fear, yawning from tension.

Earth scientists know that when a geological faultline experiences many small, 3.5 earthquakes, the pressure is released, and the likelihood of a massive, 6.5 earthquake is reduced. Social scientists like to make the same point with human behavior. When an emotion is stimulated, it needs to be discharged. Holding it in increases the internal pressure and ultimately leads to a damaging, hurtful, monstrous eruption.

The prevention of relationship rifts depends on the timely discharge of emotional conflicts. A hurt baby is not expected to hold off for a more convenient time to cry. A hurt adult retains equilibrium when he feels free to discharge his feelings at the time.

A layman, watching someone cry, is likely to say, "Look how hurt she must be, she's weeping so hard." More accurately, one might say, "She was already hurt, and crying is how she is healing herself." Stomping and raging helps us regain equilibrium after a flash of anger, shivering and shaking dispels fear, and yawning breaks tension.

Prevention is the cure may sound like a slogan, yet in relationships, learning how to be immediately responsive to conflict is a very real form of prevention. Discharging emotional tension, hurt, anger, fear, or anxiety, is a healer and dissipates the buildup of resentments that results eventually in the death of a partnership.

Men! You and I—our gender—have legendary difficulty discharging emotional tension.

When your partner walks away in anger, will you take the risk to approach her with how it makes you feel? When she is hurt by your choice of recreation (a ball game, a TV show, cards with some of your friends), instead of a shrug and a day of cold silence (your way of punishing?), will you respond to her hurt with your open thoughts and feelings? In your sexual interactions, are you willing to state openly and with vulnerability your wants or frustrations?

If you are willing to be communicative, your interest in such dialogue will trigger *her* interest in *you*. How many times have you heard a woman say, "If only he would talk to me about things"? How rare it is for that to be the man's complaint.

A good relationship begins with the prevention of behavior patterns that are inflexible and unintelligent, that gnaw at the fiber of a relationship. This means learning to be vulnerable and risk taking, aware of your own and your partner's wants, expressive and honest about your feelings, and immediately responsive to conflict.

When you have learned these skills and can use them with spontaneity, you have stored up vital energy for preventing great chasms in all your life's interactions. You will have the skills to cultivate the relationships you want.

CHAPTER TWELVE

SURPRISE

ANOTHER INDISPENSABLE VARIABLE in a successful partnership has to do with knowing how to keep things fresh and new. When you bounce back from loss, you must absorb new ways to be—new behavior, new attitudes, novel approaches to your new relationship(s)—or you will live to *repeat your old mistakes*. The element of surprise is singularly critical in a relationship that endures.

Check yourself out. Remember when you first fell in love, how it felt? The sky was bluer, the hills greener, the air fresher, poetry swelled within you, contemplating seeing your sweetheart quickened your pulse.

One man in counseling said to me, "I function best when I'm in love." And why not? You are learning someone new. Every corner you turn with her, turns you on. When you see her again after hours apart you are startled again by her beauty. Stories she tells you are novel and fresh, her style of telling them a wonder, untarnished, unsullied by a history of hurt or resentment. You can't believe your good fortune to be with such a jewel. Every moment—every anticipated moment—has attached to it the golden element of surprise.

So what happens?

Does familiarity always breed contempt? Is it inevitable for the blush to leave the rose? In man-woman relationships can the mystery stay, the initial elevation continue? In short, can the element of surprise endure? Why not?

We all have the capacity for unlimited renewal. Our prime skills are scarcely tapped, our lovingness a persistent promise which requires diligent focus. Spontaneity is part of us all in childhood; we may lose some as we get emotionally injured and more protective, but it is still there, within us, latent, available.

Psychiatrist Martin Blinder has recently written that when love fades it cannot be revived. "Once gone, romantic love is lost forever. . . . You never love the same person the same way twice." Though this may generally be the case, I have seen enough exceptions in my work with couples to proffer some hope.

Bradley was certain his wife did not love him anymore. Loving allowances had ended, the little tendernesses fled, and their sexual relationship had deteriorated progressively until it was, by the time I saw him, nonexistent. He insisted he loved her, but that she had obviously lost her desire for him. She had, in effect, already left him—emotionally.

They came in to see me separately and I asked each— without undue and unnecessary voyeurism—if they felt sexual toward others. They confessed that for a two-year period they had, as a consequence of their coldness toward each other, agreed to an open dating period. And yes, both had been able to be sexual with others.

In the safety of our therapy session, Bradley's wife told me that for the first few years of their marriage, foreplay in their sexual encounters was minimal. She did not know how to ask for more and would therefore engage in intercourse with Bradley before she was stimulated. The result was a desultory experience for her. Time after time she was disappointed in their lovemaking until she began to approach each encounter reluctantly, and eventually with disinterest.

This turned Bradley off, who said to me, "She doesn't

move, she doesn't wriggle, she doesn't come. Sex is so rotten with her, why bother. She doesn't love me."

I asked her if she loved Bradley and she answered with a shrug and a noncommittal, "I don't know."

They came in together and, with my gentle nudging, told each other their views. Bradley was completely unaware of his part in their sexual distancing. At first he seemed insulted, but later was more open and willing to self-examine.

When he saw me again alone, we worked up a personal "Surprise List" of activities he could initiate—in and out of bed—that would stir his wife's dormant feelings.

I learned long ago that I could not prescribe for my clients. What would work with one would be ineffectual with another. Bradley's surprises included:

- wearing *her* favorite men's cologne to bed
- bringing her gifts intermittently (not on a predictable schedule) and leaving them on her dresser with a card
- buying tickets periodically for a concert or stage show at the Comedy Store
- taking her out to dinner on the spur of the moment
- waking her up in the middle of the night with hugs and kisses and . . . whatever it leads to
- going to bed without pajamas on, or anything else
- climbing into bed ahead of her on *her* side of the bed and waiting for her there
- making a move on her in the kitchen or bathroom (as he did when they were first married)

I use the notion of surprise the way some think of newness. Variety as the spice of life is an accurate and valuable concept. Variety embraces newness, newness is based upon surprise.

What Bradley attempted was to renew the feeling of romance with his wife. When she was surprised by his actions, she looked at him in a new, fresh way. The tone of sameness, dullness, and predictability was removed.

Once Bradley had established curiosity in his wife, an expectation of surprise, he introduced what turned out to be the most valuable surprise of all. He approached her sexually with a whole new repertoire of preliminary movements and actions. He did his homework. He read about bedroom tactics, what to do, what to say, how to touch her, how to move, how to enhance the foreplay that would get her excited about the act of intercourse itself.

Surprise Within Routine

When we go to Universal Studios and see the *Jaws* shark, we can be thrilled by the suddenness of its attack, its difference from other animals, the fear it evokes. The same may be true for rides at Disney World or Magic Mountain, or at any country fair or circus. We seem to love being stunned or shocked, can scarcely discriminate sometimes between fear and ecstasy. The key element in our excitement seems to be surprise.

Going to an amusement park—or to a horror film, or the beach to ride monster waves—is a broad, obvious way of being stimulated. Creating surprise within the routine of everyday living is more subtle and difficult to explain and implement.

Some habitual behavior is required of us all: We brush our teeth, shave, bathe, drive our cars, do our work, wash dishes, take out the trash, pay our bills. When a couple watches television night after night, goes to bed at eleven o'clock, eats chicken every Tuesday, Italian on Thursday,

Chinese on Friday—when life in general is patterned and routine—an atrophy of spirit settles in. Activities that *might* give us choice and variety can even become dull and repetitive.

A client named Joe came to see me for a few sessions after his girlfriend dumped him with the complaint: "You're dull and predictable. There's no fire in you. Your clothes, your routine, your habits, even your name—they're all mundane!" Actually, Joe's first two names were Joseph Frederick, and after we had talked a while (he was terribly wounded and low, since this was his second failed relationship in a year) he decided some changes were in order. For one, he would begin calling himself J.F., using the initials only. "Like J.F.K.," he told me. For another, he would begin to dress differently, a difficult transition because he had been conditioned by a controlling mother to be frugal and conservative. To implement the latter, he consulted a friend whom he characterized as, "wild and a swinger, but a classy dresser."

Even more dramatic was J.F.'s change in his routine. It was risky business, he told me, to stop off at a bar with guys from the office and watch Monday Night Football, or go out on Sunday morning for brunch with friends. What feels like risk for one person is another's piece of cake.

What J.F. found was that when he made these changes, which for him represented major risks, he *felt more interesting*. And feeling that way was the first step in others seeing him that way.

When I used the word "surprise" to characterize his changes, J.F. asked me to clarify. "You introduced the element of surprise into your own life, your own way of operating," I told him. "The surprise element makes you more rare and interesting, even to yourself."

Sometimes the risky thing is to change *toward* routine. Another client, Greg, told me that women saw him as unreliable. Greg was thirty, never married, and had recently moved from New York. In his Bronx accent he said: "I can't hold on to a chick. They tell me I'm unpredictable. My last girlfriend dumped me after thirteen months—said she couldn't keep up with me, why didn't I ever want to spend a quiet evening at home?"

What worked for Greg when he was twenty and exploring, worked against him at thirty when he wanted more commitment. In the process of our counseling he began to teach himself the joys of the simple life. One day he said to me, "I'm surprising the hell out of myself. I've stayed home the last two Saturday nights. Rented movies, made myself a milkshake, kicked back. What a blast!"

Of course, two weekends do not constitute substantial personality changes. But the small adjustments Greg chose to try taught him how it felt to live differently, and since the experiences were positive, he no longer dreaded an evening alone; aloneness no longer represented being shut out or feeling like a failure.

Greg's story has a romantic ending. He was married a year later to a woman his age who had a small child. They had primary custody, and Greg discovered suddenly—the way a nonswimmer dumped in water discovers a way to paddle— how it was to be tied to a daily and nightly responsibility. His recently gained capacity to be more domestic proved to be a valuable asset.

Surprise Is More than Birthdays

It is exhilarating to be given a surprise birthday party—or anniversary, or retirement, or bon voyage party. A friend of mine was recently tricked into thinking a mutual friend was having a surprise party, when it was really for him. When everyone yelled, "Surprise!" he was so stunned he walked up to the phony party person and insisted on handing him a gift.

We all have the potential to inject the element of surprise into every day of our lives—not only party days—enriching ourselves and our partners as well. It takes both imagination and persistent awareness. Surprise is waking up on a Sunday morning and making breakfast for you and your woman—sourdough French toast sprinkled with cinnamon and caraway seeds!

Surprise is calling her in the afternoon, at work, just to say hello.

Surprise is when she says, "Why did you buy me a necklace? It isn't my birthday." And your answer, "Because I love you."

Surprise is when you tell her, "I've freed up my afternoon. I'm coming home to watch the kids so you can have some time off."

Surprise is showing up with a bottle of Chardonnay or Cabernet when she's cooking—or breaking out the fancy glasses if she brings the wine and you're cooking.

Surprise is unsolicited appreciation—for her organizing skills, her talents, her beauty, her mothering, her lovemaking.

Surprise is communicating through what you do that she is valuable, and even more gratifying, that she is enough.

Surprise is a touch on the arm as you pass her, a quick massage on the neck, tickling, playing with her fingers.

One couple I counseled were discussing touch as a symbol of affection, when the woman said, "You almost never touch me for no reason, just to show affection, to catch me by surprise. I don't get enough touch from you." Her man replied:

"What have you got, a touch parking meter?" "No, but if I did," she said sardonically, "it would always be in the red."

This couple struggled in joint therapy for six months and then one evening the woman said to me, "He's fine in bed, but he doesn't know how to hold my hand." A week later she decided on divorce.

Surprise in a relationship is most of all an indication of freedom of spirit. The most common complaint of women in couples therapy is that they feel they have lost their freedom. They have become helpless, dependent, their spirit squelched. When a partnership becomes occluded by resentment, the element of surprise is squeezed out of it. Freedom to innovate, to be creative within the routine or in lovemaking, is stifled.

Freedom and surprise nurture each other. Surprise moments enhance the feeling of freedom, corroborate the free choices we all have before hurt and resentment chiseled them down; freedom of spirit allows the surprise genie to run wild with unfettered imagination.

Of all the factors that go into the positive percolating of a relationship, *fresh appreciation* for your partner seems to me to be of premier importance. The desire for surprise—or novelty, or variety—seems deeply ingrained in us all. It is probably the primary reason for sexual promiscuity. There is a mandate, therefore, if a partnership is to survive, to keep that element of surprise cooking within the relationship, so that one is not tempted to look elsewhere to find it.

All honeymoons come to an end. Though courts talk about no- fault divorce, the real no-fault divorce can lie only in the perceptions of the participants. You take on a positive, optimistic life stance again when you give up blaming and finger-pointing. The idea of no fault offers a profound free-dom to get on with your life without the shackles of resentment and vindictiveness. New relationships will require similar, healthy, diligent care.

Now, in the final chapter coming up, it is time to sum up, to scrutinize those who have bounced back from a lost love and found new meaning in their lives. What are they like? What are their prospects? Are you one of them?

CHAPTER THIRTEEN

AN INVINCIBLE SUMMER

To be free—to be able to stand up and leave everything behind without looking back—to say yes.

—DAG HAMMERSKJOLD

THOSE OF US WHO HAVE BEEN left by others must and do cultivate a sixth sense. The seeds may have been sown by fear, and irrigated by caution, but they are nourished by the hope that our harvest will be a new love born of awareness and wisdom. For one, we tend to recognize each other. The characteristics of our pain (on the recovery trail) have gouged lasting furrows in our manner, style, personality, and in how we carry ourselves—our walk, our posture, our look. Now, we "know when to hold 'em and know when to fold 'em"—we are not about to let the same thing happen again.

It has been over a dozen years since my marriage ended. My children are grown, healthy, and flourishing, and my interaction with my former wife is cordial and supportive. Our contacts principally concern the children, but we belong to some professional groups together, sponsor many of the same causes, and see each other regularly at birthdays and holidays.

The hurt of our divorce remains an unspoken splinter of contention between us—but we are able to see that *she* is okay and *I* am okay, and it was the mix that could no longer be sustained.

Curiously enough, neither of us has remarried, an unusual statistic in America's divorce scene.

Quentin and Paul, two men whose women left them, are now also fully functioning in their new lives. Their losses, like a receding landscape, have slid away into the distance, the exorcism of pain and resentment aided by new perspectives and new relationships.

What I am struck with most about men who successfully negotiate recovery is how mellow and self-revealing they can become. One man communicated this partially by the button he had pinned to his shirt. It read: "If you really want to know me, please hear what I'm not saying." He also told me that his ex was in a new relationship, that he had met the man, and that—grand achievement!—he liked him.

It is gratifying to see how accurate our perceptions can be, and how men and women can become sensitive observers of the divorce (and recovery) process—"experts on their own intimacy," as I said in the Preface.

Paul wrote a piece for his community's newspaper which they published. With his consent, the vignette is presented here.

OMELET: AMERICAN STYLE

There's a place out in the Valley that's famous for its omelets, and there I sat, cool and detached, watching Sunday morning develop. Watching men, actually, in a curious tableau that made a startlingly clear and painful comment about America's changed social structure.

There were four altogether. The first one I noticed was full-bearded and wore a blue jogging suit with white stripes. His youngster was barely past infancy and sat in a chrome-trayed high chair to his left, dropping bits of toast on the carpet as fast as the man replaced them. He seemed perplexed by the child's persistence, but equally determined. No easy task, this separate parenting, this split-time role-reversal.

Women have started to make the moves and men are struggling to cope. Used to be that a man in his thirties would get itchy feet and a roving eye, pick up a swift sports car and sign into a swinging bachelor pad down at the beach. But now sports cars are unisex, the water-front apartments as populated by the "little woman" as by the "old man"—all having a fling at life before it's too late.

The second man who caught my attention took a table directly across from mine. He was gray at the temples and gabbed earnestly with his young son. The boy was intent on his bacon and eggs, yet clearly relished his dad's exclusive attention. I caught snatches of the dialogue.

"So what did you do in school? Anything exciting?"

"I don't know."

"I mean did you do any new things?"

"Not really."

"What about your enrichment class? You were doing something with plants, weren't you?"

"That was last term."

"Oh."

Old stuff—two, three, four days old or more. Bor-ing. The boy responded reluctantly, sparingly. The father had a curious twist to his mouth. So painful, so awkward, this pulling for information. How natural it

155

used to be at home to share the day's events, off-
handedly, easily, no big deal. But now, how humbling,
how contrived.

The third man was shepherding a family of three—
a teenaged daughter and two younger sons. The girl
appeared sullen, angry.

"Why do we have to go out to breakfast?"

"Well, we don't *have* to. It's one chance for us to get
together."

"You make me come."

"I don't make you come, but I'm glad you do. You
aren't forced. . . ."

He suffered, this third one. His sons watched him
askance, sensing down deep somehow his pain and his
need. How logical and simple to confront a sassy
teenager at home, in the family—and now, how fragile,
how careful. Now, how reluctant to risk her ire—and
how quick she is to see his vulnerability.

The fourth father came in with two little girls and wore
a boating cap. The girls did not resemble him, and I tried
to imagine what their mother looked like. Of the four,
he was the jauntiest—independent and flip. The wrin-
kles had been ironed out. His new life was already working for him. Two years past dissolution was my best guess.

And the one with the taciturn son—about a year past.

And the bearded cat with the baby—a few short months.

And the father of three—well, maybe only separated,
the break still fresh and raw.

Each one chafing in a clear, distinct stage in the ongoing process called marital dissolution, American style.
Almost predictable as heat in August: disbelief, desperation, depression, anger, resentment, resignation, and, at
long last, a kind of regeneration, a rebirth.

As I sank deeper into my analysis, my companion nudged me.

"Let's go," he said.

"Yeah, sure." I left the tip and checked out, bidding a silent adieu to the four stalwart trailblazers.

As we left, my companion reminded me, "Don't forget, my Little League game's tomorrow at 4:30, Dad."

Cool, compromising, adjusted to periodic rendezvous, I assured him: "Sure, Son. I'll be there."

I'm three years past.

Not all my bouncing-back clients land on such elevated plateaus of understanding. In some ways Paul is atypical— but in other ways his tale is universal.

Certainly, common themes run through every case I have cited. They start with the recognition that when a relationship fails, *men hurt too*. And they conclude with a kind of national anthem for all who struggle to bounce back from the loss of a love. Here are the major lyrics:

LIFE IS WHAT YOU MAKE IT

Your life does not end because someone in it drops out of it;

Change is resisted and painful, yet new patterns of satisfaction and joy will emerge;

A partnership may fail, but you are not a failure;

There is no fault, there is no blame—and yet you are responsible for yourself;

You would do well to remember what every child learns at a young age:

Flush!—You regain balance and health when you discharge the waste products of pain and resentment.

From recovering people I have gained many new insights, perhaps the most important being: If I or some institution rescue you from your "downer" or loss or disappointment, you will have stored up no resources for solving the next and the next life crisis. The recovery process is most life-enhancing when you are aware that *you* have been the source of your own heat and light and strength. You are on your way when you finally learn that there is in you ". . . an invincible summer."

I wrote the following verse to end this hopeful odyssey along the serpentine trail of recovery from the loss of a relationship. It is a statement and a plea.

THINK KINDLY ON THE MAN . . .

Think kindly on the man who's lost
His wife or POSSLQ*
He's shed his credibility,
His social life's a zoo.

Before he was a humanist
Congruent and serene,
Till caught in the dehumanizing
Swinging singles scene.
"A partnership can never last
Forever and a day.
You're free—so live it up, old boy,"
His single friends all say.

But being free can be a drag,
There's no stability.
Some dates are blind and some the kind
That tax civility.

158

It's women who are prone to label
Man a parasite.
"They only want a single thing
Then thank you, Ma'am, good night."

But men can crave relationships
As much as women do,
And suffer when they terminate
And miss their partners too.

Degrading when they're on display
With fancy clothes and cars—
A unisex ignominy
This hanging out in bars.

It's time to think androgyny,
It's time to change the view;
Think kindly on the man who's lost
His wife or POSSLQ.*

*Persons Of Opposite Sex Sharing Living Quarters

Oh, the comfort, the inexpressible comfort of feeling safe with a person; having neither to weigh thought nor measure words, but pouring them all right out, just as they are, chaff and grain together; certain that a faithful hand will take and sift them, keep what is worth keeping, and with a breath of kindness, blow the rest away.

—SHOSHONE INDIANS

SUGGESTED READINGS

Some Sources on Divorce

Adam, John, and Nancy Adam. *Divorce: How and When to Let Go.* Englewood Cliffs, NJ: Prentice-Hall, 1979.

Bohannan, Paul., ed. *Divorce and After.* Garden City, NY: Doubleday, 1978.

Colgrove, Melba, Harold H. Bloomfield and Peter McWilliams. *How to Survive the Loss of a Love: 58 Things to Do When There is Nothing to Be Done.* New York: Lion Press; Distributed by Simon and Schuster, 1976.

Duncan, Roger T., and Darlene Duncan. *You're Divorced, But Your Children Aren't.* Englewood Cliffs, NJ: Prentice-Hall, 1979.

Gardner, Richard. *The Boys and Girls Book About Divorce.* New York: Bantam Books, 1970.

Gardner, Richard. *The Parents Book About Divorce.* New York: Bantam Books, 1979.

Hunt, Morton, and Bernice Hunt. *The Divorce Experience.* New York: McGraw-Hill, 1978.

Kessler, Sheila. *The American Way of Divorce: Prescription for Change.* Chicago: Nelson-Hall, 1975.

Rice, J.K., and D.G. Rice. *Living Through Divorce.* New York: Guilford Press, 1986.

Sheresky, Norman, and Marya Mannes. *Uncoupling: The Art of Coming Apart.* New York: Viking Press, 1972.

Trafford, Abigail. *Crazy Time: Surviving Divorce.* New York: Harper and Row, 1982.

Wallerstein, Judith S., and Joan Berlin Kelly. *Surviving the BreakUp: How Children and Parents Cope with Divorce.* New York: Basic Books, 1980.

Weitzman, Lenore. *The Divorce Revolution: The Unexpected Social and Economic Consequences for Women and Children in America.* New York: Free Press, 1985.

Some Sources on Divorce and Recovery

Alvarez, A. *Life After Marriage: Love in an Age of Divorce.* New York: Simon and Schuster, 1981.

Fisher, Bruce. *Rebuilding: When Your Relationship Ends.* San Luis Obispo, CA: Impact Publ., 1981.

Galper, Miriam. *Co-Parenting: Sharing Your Child Equally.* Philadelphia: Running Press, 1978.

Johnson, Stephen. *First Person Singular: Living the Good Life Alone.* New York: Signet Books, 1977.

Krantzer, Mel. *Learning to Love Again.* New York: Crowell Co., 1977.

Napolitane, Catherine, and Victoria Pellegrino. *Learning and Loving After Divorce.* New York: The New American Library, 1977.

Nichols, William. "Divorce and Remarriage Education." *Journal of Divorce* I, 2 (Winter 1977): 153-161.

Turrow, Rita. *Daddy Doesn't Live Here Anymore.* New York: Anchor Books, 1978.

Some Sources on Mediation

Blades, Joan. *Family Mediation: Cooperative Divorce Settlement.* Englewood Cliffs, NJ: Prentice-Hall, 1985.

Haynes, John M. *Divorce Mediation: A Practical Guide for Therapists and Counselors.* New York: Spring Publishing Co., 1981.

Irving, Howard H. *Divorce Mediation: A Rational Alternative to the Adversary System.* New York: Universe Books, 1981.

Kressel, Kenneth. *The Process of Divorce: How Professionals and Couples Negotiate Settlements.* New York: Basic Books, 1985.

Some Sources Primarily for Men

Ferrara, Frank. *On Being Father: A Divorced Man Talks About Sharing the New Responsibilities of Parenthood.* Garden City, NY: Doubleday, 1985.

Gatley, Richard H., and David Koulack. *Single Father's Handbook.* Garden City, NY: Anchor Press/Doubleday, 1979.

Hallberg, Edmond C. *The Gray Itch.* Briarcliff Manor, NY: Stein and Day, 1977.

Jacobs, John W., ed. *Divorce and Fatherhood: The Struggle For Parental Identity.* Washington, DC: American Psychiatric Press, 1986.

Levinson, Daniel J. *The Seasons of a Man's Life.* New York: Ballantine Books, 1978.

Silver, Gerald A., and Myrna Silver. *Weekend Fathers.* Los Angeles: Stratford Press; Distributed by Harper and Row, 1981.

Some Support Groups

The Coalition of Free Men. P.O. Box 129, Manhasset, NY 11030.

Family Rights and Responsibilities. 34421 Harrah Rd., Aqua Dulce, CA. 91350.

Father's Aid of San Diego. P.O. Box 80914, San Diego, CA. 92138.

Father's Rights of America, Inc. P.O. Box 7596, Van Nuys, CA. 91409.

National Congress For Men. 14661 Sherwood Court, Oak Park, MI. 48237.

Parents Sharing Custody. 18401 Burbank Blvd., Tarzana, CA. 91356.

Positive Divorce Institute. (Kelly and Cogan: Attorneys and Counselors at Law.) 2632 Lincoln Blvd., Santa Monica, CA. 90405.

Newer Releases

Adler, Allan J., M.D., and Christine Archambault. *Divorce Recovery: Healing the Hurt Through Self-Help and Professional Support.* New York: Bantam Books, 1992.

Belli, Melvin, and Mel Krantzler. *Divorcing.* New York: St. Martin's Press, 1988. Legal and emotional advice on the divorce process.

Felder, Leonard. *A Fresh Start.* New York: Signet, 1987. How to let go of emotional baggage and enjoy your life again.

Gullo, Stephen, and Connie Church. *Loveshock: How to Recover From a Broken Heart and Love Again.* New York: Simon and Schuster, 1988.

Kingma, Daphne Rose. *Coming Apart: Why Relationships End and How to Live Through the Ending of Yours.* New York: Ballantine Books, 1987.

Penney, Alexandra, *Why Men Stray and Why Men Stay.* New York: Bantam Books, 1989.

Shapiro, Joan, M.D., in collaboration with George Hartlaub, M.D., *Men: A Translation for Women.* New York: Dutton Books, 1992.

About the Author

Stan Charnofsky played baseball and managed in the New York Yankees organization for seven years before beginning his second career as a California State University at Northridge professor of Educational Psychology and Counseling in 1961.

Dr. Charnofsky, who won the 1989 CSUN Distinguished Teaching Award, now chairs the Department of Educational Psychology and Counseling. Over the past twenty years, he has designed courses in his specialty, marriage and family counseling, and conducted workshops on relationships, how to sustain them, what happens when they come apart, and how to learn to love again.

Dr. Charnofsky is also the author of *Educating the Powerless* (Wadsworth Publishing, 1971). He has lectured throughout the United States, Canada, and Israel, and he has been featured in numerous articles and publications.

New World Library is dedicated to publishing books and cassettes that help improve the quality of our lives.

For a catalog of our fine books and cassettes, contact:
  New World Library
  58 Paul Drive
  San Rafael, CA 94903
  Phone: (415) 472-2100
  FAX: (415) 472-6131

Or call toll free:
  (800) 227-3900
  In Calif.: (800) 632-2122